IVORY TOWERS
AND DRESSED STONES

Andy Wibbe
L'pool ox/16

Castle Hill near Huddersfield

IVORY TOWERS AND DRESSED STONES

Exploring the Follies, Prospect Towers & other Curiosities of Northern England
Vol 2: Yorkshire

by Jim Jarratt

CICERONE PRESS,
MILNTHORPE, CUMBRIA

For
THE YOMPERS
Trish, Richard, Jaimie Lou and Lawly Liz

ACKNOWLEDGEMENTS

Special thanks to: Mr Keith Povey and Mr Ken Plant, for supplying
me with the work (ie. income) necessary to bring this project to a
successful conclusion. To Mr Peter J.Ainscough, Humberside County
Librarian, and Miss P.Martin, Humberside Libraries and Arts Unit;
to Mrs J.Hodge, Huddersfield Librarian; to Mr Steve Burnip at YTV
and to the Independent Broadcasting Authority for information on
Emley Moor.

Advice to Readers

Readers are advised that whilst every effort is taken by the author to
ensure the accuracy of this guidebook, changes can occur which may
affect the contents. It is advisable to check locally on transport,
accommodation, shops etc but even rights-of-way can be altered and,
more especially overseas, paths can be eradicated by landslip, forest fires
or changes of ownership.

The publisher would welcome notes of any such changes

Front cover: Boot's Folly, Strines

CONTENTS

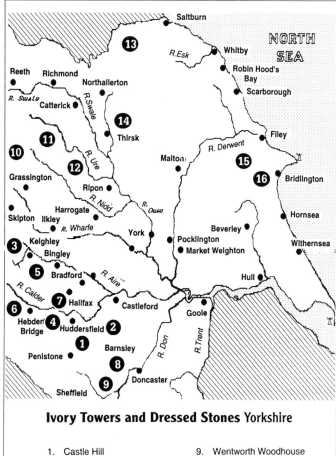

Ivory Towers and Dressed Stones Yorkshire

INTRODUCTION

"Folly" - "a useless and needlessly extravagant structure". So says the dictionary. "Extravagant" perhaps, but only "useless" in the very strictest of terminologies, for how can something that brings pleasure, delight and fascination, and which stretches our imagination and offers a fine prospect of the landscape be "useless"? Follies are a joy. Obscure and mysterious, they create a mythology that is entirely their own. Often in connection with them we hear stories of eccentric and quirky human behaviour which are sometimes factual... and sometimes not! Above all, these structures are shrines to the cult of the rugged individualist, and are representative of the human need to leave one's mark upon the landscape in a fantasy of "Ivory Towers and Dressed Stones".

This book is essentially a collection of rambles based around follies. My main object has been the satisfaction of a long held curiosity. On seeing a folly the questions on most people's lips are "How do I get to it?" "Why was it built?" and "Who built it?" This book aims to answer some of these questions, and also to offer some enjoyable and informative rambles into the bargain. Each folly visited in this volume is incorporated into a circular walk based on your parked car. The walks are all free... free access, free parking. It is an annoyance to me to have to fork out for the privilege of enjoying the countryside, so I have based my walks only around those places which enjoy free access.

Each walk contains, in addition to the follies, general historical and topographical information and detailed commentary concerning places of interest encountered en route, together with "how to get there" information, and detailed, hand drawn maps. Where rambles are suitable for small children this is noted.

Follies visited in this book fall into two distinct types. First are the "prospect towers", most commonly to be found on Pennine hilltops. These usually contain a staircase leading to a lookout point from which visitors may enjoy the view, which is, of course their raison d'être, despite usually being constructed on the pretext of commemorating some famous (or not so famous) person and/or event. Our second type of folly is the "topographical curiosity".

Mock ruins and sham castles fall into this category, along with bogus "prehistoric hill figures" and standing stones, grottoes, temples and pyramids. Many of these are to be found in the parklands and estates of great houses.

One of the greatest pleasures of my folly hunting expeditions has been the topographical correlation of one walk with another. From Castle Hill, Huddersfield, for example,you can see Stoodley Pike. From Stoodley Pike you can see Wainhouse Tower etc. You will soon find that the visiting of follies not only broadens your knowledge of the curious and the obscure, but will also contribute to your understanding of the landscapes and topography of Northern England.

Follies are like white elephants. Some of them are put on show to the public, some are stuffed and preserved, but by far the majority of them are left to rot and decay in that great elephant's graveyard of Private Property. If they were mediaeval castles or Roman remains the Department of the Environment would protect and restore them as part of our national heritage, and open them up to the public, but being mere follies they are left to crumble away in overgrown obscurity. Many are lost forever, (the Ladies Folly at Tankersley Park is a good example) and others are well on the way to dust and oblivion. The greatest enemy to the survival of the folly is our ignorance of its existence, and if this book can do even a little towards dispelling that darkness and instilling an interest and enthusiasm where previously there was none, then that alone will have served a useful and worthwhile purpose.

Follies are mysterious and inscrutable. They also have an infinite variety. Some of them will be found on the "beaten track" while others you will find to be secluded and hard of access. In some cases the folly is the centrepiece of an average ramble, while in others it takes second place to an excellent walk. Sometimes you will get the best of both. The landscapes visited range from white limestone uplands to sombre Pennine moors, from the Cleveland Hills to the Dark Peak. When you have undertaken all the days out featured in this book you will have sampled a slice of virtually every landscape in Yorkshire. All you need is a car, good boots and a desire to seek out the odd and the unusual. This book will do the rest.

ABOUT THE FOLLIES

This book does not purport to be exhaustive! To create a series of rambles which visited every folly in Northern England would result in a ridiculously large volume. I have had to leave many follies out, so many in fact, that I felt obliged to suggest further options for the would-be-folly hunter. I have done this by placing an appendix - a kind of mini gazetteer of follies - at the end of the book. Not all of the follies mentioned there have been visited, and there is scope for the reader to make his or her own explorations and discoveries as I did. My reasons for missing out the follies contained in these appendices have been varied. Some are sited in predominantly urban areas which offer little scope for the rambler. Some are on "Private Property", and may (or may not!) be accessible to the public on payment of an appropriate entrance fee.

Some follies are dangerous (Mowbray Point at Hackfall is a good example). Rusty nails in fallen beams can pierce even the stoutest boot, and the dangers of rotten floors and crumbling masonry should be palpably and appallingly obvious. By all means explore - but if you must err, err on the side of safety. Broken in boots are permissible, broken in heads are not!

You will find that few of the walks in this book are especially difficult. On some the countryside is the main draw, on others the rogue architecture. Sometimes we get both. Writing this book was for myself and my family an adventure. Hopefully my readers will, using the information, be able to continue from where I left off. I will detain you no longer, the vast and varied landscape of England's largest county awaits.

Oliver Duckett, Gilling. (see p156)

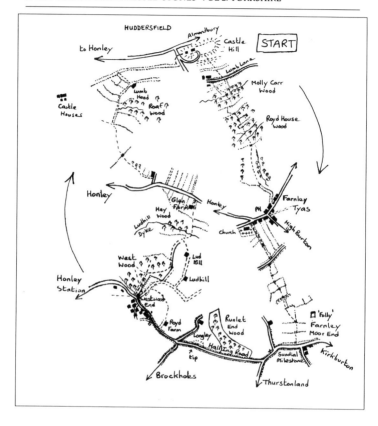

Description of route in *italics*

Star Rating

* Fair
** Good
*** Very Good

West Riding

1: CASTLE HILL AND FARNLEY TYAS

"Last of the Summer Wine" landscapes, the remains of an Iron Age hillfort and a Norman castle, and a fine prospect tower make an exciting start to this pleasant walk through pastures and woodlands within a stone's throw of urban Huddersfield.

Getting there:	From Huddersfield town centre follow the A629 Sheffield Road for about ½ mile. Beyond two sets of lights, ascending the hill take the filter off to the right (signed Almondbury). Proceed up Almondbury Bank, which leads steeply up to Almondbury Village. Just beyond the church turn right into Westgate and passing a fine old half timbered house, follow the lane out of the village, passing through a residential area until countryside is reached at Ashes Common Farm (on left). Continue onwards, passing Castle Hill on the left, until reaching the next junction of roads. Turn left onto Lumb Lane, and about 100 yards on a narrow metalled lane leads off left, winding up the southern face of Castle Hill to the car park on the summit. Parking is ample and free!
Distance:	6 miles. Moderate.
Map ref:	SE 153 141 Huddersfield Sheet 102 (1") or Pathfinder Huddersfield & Marsden
Rating:	Walk *** General Interest ***

When you get out of your car and wander around the pleasant green sward of Castle Hill, strolling along earthen ramparts and enjoying the fine views of urban Huddersfield below, nestling at the junction of the Colne and Holme Valleys, you will quickly realise that here is a site of great historical significance. Like The Trundle at Goodwood in Sussex, or the famous Maiden Castle in Dorset, Castle Hill is unmistakably a prehistoric hillfort.

The general consensus among antiquarians is that the earthworks on Castle Hill were constructed around 300 BC. Covering eight acres, and standing on a 900 feet bluff, the fortifications must have been formidable indeed. The original works consisted of a single stone rampart and a rock cut ditch across the southern end of the hill. Later, the rampart was doubled and extended around the entire hilltop. Finally the whole camp was enclosed by a huge outer earthwork.

That the hillfort was constructed by the Brigantian inhabitants of Iron Age Yorkshire is in no doubt. Beyond that, we must speculate. In Ptolemy's map of the world, which was compiled around AD 160, a place by the name of Camulodunum is shown about fifty miles southwest of Eboracum (York), and it seems possible that Castle Hill was the place to which he referred.

With the conquest of Britain by the Romans, Castle Hill was abandoned. The Romans had their military highway and fort at Slack (see walk 4), and the fortifications were of no use to them. Throughout the Dark Ages the hill remained untenanted, until a few years after the Norman Conquest, when the powerful Norman De Lacy Family saw it as a ready made site for the construction of a motte and bailey type castle to dominate the surrounding countryside.

The castle consisted of three wards, the outer bailey, an inner bailey (where the present Castle Hotel now stands) and an inner ward, where the Jubilee Tower is now situated on the site of the Norman keep. To the south of the keep a deep Norman well was sunk, which may still be inspected today. The castle was probably erected during the reign of Stephen, but as early as 1340 it is recorded as being ruinous. Its history was fairly uneventful, but it is recorded that in 1307 a jury was set up to investigate certain happenings in the castle, where it was alleged that "a certain stranger had been murdered in the dungeons and his body thrown outside, that his body when discovered was 'a complete mass of corruption' as if it had been 'devoured by worms, birds and dogs'".

By Elizabethan times the site of the keep had become the site of a beacon. Here was lit the cresset which warned of the sighting of the Spanish Armada in 1588. A contemporary document informs us that: "Halifax Beacon giveth light to the beacon of Ryney (Reevy) within Bradford, and receiveth light from Castle Hill Beacon nigh Almondbury. It may be seen at Blackstone Edge and Pomfrett." The Napoleonic Wars too saw the beacon in use, but by the end of the nineteenth century it had become little more than a memory.

Finally, in 1898 the Victoria (Jubilee) Tower was built on the site, to celebrate the Diamond Jubilee of Queen Victoria. When the foundations for this structure were being dug out in 1897 the dungeons of the old keep were brought to light. Unfortunately they were filled in with rubble and now lie lost beneath tons of heavy Victorian masonry. The tower, standing almost 100 feet high, was built by public subscription, the foundation stone being laid by Mr John Frecheville Ramsden, son of the illustrious Sir John Ramsden, who was responsible for Huddersfield's canal link to the sea. The tower is open to the public on bank holidays and summer weekends, and a small admission charge enables you to enjoy the fine view from the windswept battlements and to browse around the small interpretive museum inside.

Another, more recent, inscription set into the masonry of this tower informs us that:

> The lantern on this tower was bought with
> public subscriptions to an appeal by
> Huddersfield Civic Society to commemorate
> the Silver Jubilee of Queen Elizabeth II
> 1952-1977.
> Kirklees Metropolitan Council
> Councillor J. Brooke
> Mayor

One of the nice things about visiting a folly is being able to pinpoint other follies. Admiring the view from the Jubilee Tower you are spoiled for choice! To the NW the Wainhouse Tower can be seen poking its head out from Calderdale and to the left of that Stoodley Pike Monument is in view. Nearer at hand, above the Colne Valley, the Nab End Tower may be seen on its buttress of rock

The Jubilee Tower

outcrops. In the opposite direction the Emley Moor Mast is quite unmissable, but a closer scrutiny will be required to pinpoint the Whitley Moor Gazebo. Now it is time to descend from Castle Hill and to proceed upon our walk.

Start from car park by the Castle Hotel. Cross the access road and follow a path along the castle earthworks until a path is seen leading off to the right down the slope. After descending a short distance turn left, following a path between hawthorn and holly trees to a stile, beyond which a field path leads down to a lane. Cross the lane to a stile opposite then proceed down pasture to another stile. Ignore the path leading off right to The Lumb, and continue straight on, descending the pasture to Lumb Lane. Cross to a signed stile opposite (near a seat) and continue onwards to the next hedge. Follow the hedge to the right for a short distance, and when the path from The Lumb appears on the right, turn sharp left, descending steps to Molly Carr Wood, crossing Lumb Dike by a plank bridge.

Follow the path out of the woods, crossing another field before entering Royd House Wood through a most attractive stone stile. Proceed through woods, crossing a short "corridor" of pasture before entering more woodlands and crossing a couple of small watercourses. On leaving the woods proceed up the steep pasture, with a scrub choked watercourse on the left, to a gate. Bear left, then right, following the track up to Farnley Tyas. On reaching the road, turn right into the village, passing the Golden Cock Inn on the right. Ignore the road leading off to Highburton, and continue onwards to the church.

Farnley Tyas derives its name from the Tyas Family, who were ancient lords of Woodsome. The name is recorded in the Almondbury area as early as the thirteenth century. According to one source the name appears as "Teutonicus" on Latin deeds, which suggests that the Tyas's were a family of German origin. In the thirteenth century Roger of Notton granted Farnley and Woodsome to Baldwin Tyas, and Sir Baldwin and his heirs were to rule over Farnley and Woodsome for many years, their estates eventually passing to the Finchenden and Kaye Families.

Modern Farnley betrays little of these knightly origins. Its church, unusually dedicated to St Lucius, was built in 1840. There is a pleasant pub, the Golden Cock, where a drink may be enjoyed whilst sitting in the sun, although the atmosphere seems somehow alien to ramblers.

Folly near Storthes Hall

Just before reaching the church a signed path leads off to the left, down the side of the churchyard. This becomes a track between walls and holly bushes, finally diminishing to a path which enters a metalled lane. Cross to the stile opposite, from which a path leads through a succession of stiles, passing a curious Folly in the arable field to the left before entering Greenside Road at Farnley Moor End. This red brick tower, almost Babylonian in appearance, is a structure of unknown origin. It appears to have been some kind of a pumping station associated with nearby Storthes Hall Hospital. It seems unlikely it was built as a folly, but a quick and unofficial visit satisfied me that whatever the building's function once was, it no longer fulfils it. A brick hole in its concrete floor is now filled with rubble and the building is in a ruinous condition. If it wasn't a folly, it certainly is one now!

A right turn leads along Greenside Road to a junction of roads, the tall spire of Thurstonland Church now prominently in view. At this junction is a unique milestone. The Huddersfield area is well endowed with these old wayside guide stoops, usually carved during the eighteenth century out of local stone, betraying the fact that the peaceful and remote lanes on which they are generally sited were once major thoroughfares. The guide stoop at Greenside Road End is unusual in that it incorporates a sundial. An appropriate crudely carved inscription informs us that that the milestone/sundial was erected by:

> JO:n Hoyle
> CONSTABLE
> Tho: BOTHOmly
> SURVEYOR/ 1738.

The other faces of the stone, adorned with pointing hands, inform us of the distances to Huddersfield, Honley, Holmfirth and "Pennyftone".

From the milestone our route leads along Hall-Ing Road to Longley Hill, with fine views of the "Summer Wine" country opening up before us. Descend to the crossroads just below Longley, and continue onwards, passing Royd Farm on the right and descending through housing before entering path into West Wood on the right.

Ascend through woods, ignoring paths off to the left, until the path enters a pasture, becoming a "causeyed" path running around the base of Lud Hill. After a succession of stiles the path reaches the head of Ludhill Dyke, and then, after a short series of steps leads through pastures to enter the Honley Road just beyond Glen Farm.

Turn left along Honley Road for about ¹/₄ mile, before turning right up the track to Farnley Hey. Just before reaching buildings, pass through the stile on the left and follow an indistinct path through open fields, following line of trees. On reaching a gate near some concrete buildings, continue onwards, bearing slightly right, to a stile in the wall. Do not continue onwards to Castle Houses, but instead turn right, following a wall to a stile by a wood (steep ravine in woodland on the right). Continue onwards to a gate, and then (with a wall on the left) onwards to the next field boundary. Turn left up the wallside then turn right onto the track which leads from Castle Houses to Lumb Lane. On reaching a metalled road turn left, and follow the road round the face of Castle Hill. Turn right up steps to the Jubilee Tower and a well deserved pint in the Castle Hotel!

Now, tired and sitting in the sun, and no doubt refreshed by a pint from pub, you can relax a little and allow your imagination to wander before you "up stumps" and risk your car on the steep descent down to Lumb Lane.

There is ample scope for your imagination. We have touched on the sober history of Castle Hill but not at all on the wealth of legends that are attached to it. Castle Hill is a place of mystery. Its earmarking as the probable site of "Camulodunum" has raised rather more romantic speculation that it might be the site of Arthur's "Camelot". The more sober appraisal suggests that the name was derived from "Camulos" a Celtic Deity corresponding to Mars, the Roman God of War, but despite this the Arthurian Association exists. According to Camden, who wrote in 1586, Castle Hill was the site of a Roman fort and a Saxon cathedral where Paulinus preached, both of which have been disproved by modern archaeology.

There are, however, stranger stories. Mediaeval sources mention a portion of the hill known as "Wormcliffe", suggesting the one time existence of a dragon. (From the Anglo Saxon "wyrm", meaning a dragon.) Dragons in Anglo-Saxon times were associated with death and burial, and it could be that the "Wormcliffe" in question was in fact an Anglo-Saxon burial ground, where Saxon cinerary urns were adorned with "wyrm" symbols. Of course you could speculate that a dragon (along with King Arthur's Knights), sleeps beneath the hill... but that's up to you!

Needless to say, where there are dragons, there is treasure for them to stand guard over. Children in Almondbury were once rocked to sleep with stories about "'t' Golden Cradle". This treasure is supposed to be hidden in one of Castle Hill's ditches, but no-one seems to know where or why. No doubt it is stashed away in one of the many tunnels which are believed to honeycomb the hill. When the "Castle Tavern" was constructed in 1812 the remains of "a winding subterranean staircase" were discovered. Whether or not this was explored is not related. It conveniently disappeared beneath the foundations of the pub!

Legends persist of a great battle fought on Castle Hill, but the origins of this tale are more likely to be found in the long running feud between the Beaumont and Kaye families, which resulted in a bloody skirmish at nearby Hall Bower in 1471 and in the death of Nicholas Beaumont of Newsome. The Beaumonts were also involved in the infamous "Elland Feud" over in Calderdale, a medieval vendetta between local families which piled tragedy upon tragedy..... they must have been hard to get along with!

So, as kids play football, or fly kites, adults picnic or descend on the Castle Hotel. Recently a beacon was lit here for the Armada Celebrations of 1988. In the last century the hill was a venue for the rather less savoury pursuits of dog fighting, cockfighting and bareknuckle prizefighting. Today it is still one of the major recreation areas for the people of Huddersfield. They would be hard put to find a finer one. With velvet turf, a pub, superb sweeping views and a lookout tower, Castle Hill must be one of the the most interesting "public parks" in England!

2: THE DUMB STEEPLE AND
THE WHITLEY MOOR GAZEBO

Two mysterious follies - a "Dumb Steeple" and a "Devil's Tower", coniferous forest, sweeping views and the remains of coal mining characterise this fine upland walk, the high point (literally), being a close encounter with Yorkshire's greatest "Prospect Tower", Emley Moor TV Transmitter.

Getting there:	From Huddersfield follow A629 Sheffield Road southwards. Pass The Tolson Museum on the right and continue onwards to the junction of the Wakefield and Sheffield Roads. Take the left fork, following the A642 Wakefield Road uphill through Lepton. At the crossroads, where the A637 leads off right to Flockton, turn left onto the B6118 Brighouse Road. Grange Moor is approximately 1/4 mile along this road. Turn right and park in village.
Distance:	8 miles approx. A fair hike
Map ref:	SE 222 160 Landranger 110
Rating:	Walk *** General Interest ***

Grange Moor is a "pit village" of a place. Sited on the high upland area which lies twixt Huddersfield and Wakefield it is part Pennine in character and part coalfield. Certainly it is lofty enough. Views around here tend to be sweeping. The fact that the landscape is a domesticated one, lacking the open moorland prevalent to the west of Huddersfield does not reduce its basic bleakness in any way. The pastures hereabouts may be green, but the winds blow just as chill over this raw landscape as they do on the high Pennine moors.

Grange Moor is a pit village of the past. Collieries abound hereabouts on the maps, but find them on the ground if you can! Their existence is simply due to the maps being out of date. Today there are only a few pits left in this area. One is the Denby Grange Colliery, a massive mining undertaking with entrances all around

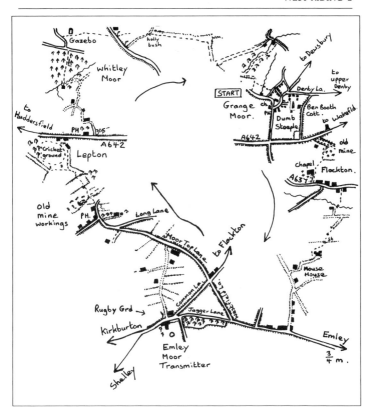

the area, another is Caphouse Colliery, about two miles down the main road, which is now open to the public as the Yorkshire Mining Museum. Otherwise Grange Moor is left alone with its memories.

Our walk starts by the playground. Proceed through the village towards Dewsbury. Turn right down Steeple Avenue (cul-de-sac). At the end of the avenue turn left down the snicket to observe the Dumb Steeple in a small pasture.

The Dumb Steeple is tucked away in a field behind Grange Moor, surrounded by chicken runs and council houses. The stone slab set into this curious gritstone structure informs us that the landmark was:

Rebuilt
By Richard
:H: Beau:
mont ——
Eʃqire
1766.

The inscription makes it obvious that there was a "Dumb Steeple" on this spot prior to 1766, but reveals nothing as to its nature or purpose. That it is a folly is in no doubt, it being an absurdly pointless structure. Richard Beaumont was one of a long line of Beaumonts who were squires of the Whitley Beaumont Estates, centred on Whitley Hall. Perhaps the reason for his building this odd cone was simply that the old one had been struck by lightning and needed replacement. But what then was the purpose of the original Steeple? We can only speculate.

Its curious name may offer some clues. The Dumb Steeple is not unique. There is another "Dumb Steeple" not too far distant, which stands alongside the busy main road from Brighouse to Mirfield, near Colne Bridge (see Appendix). This is a well known landmark,

Dumb Steeple
Mirfield

being the place from which the Luddites set out to attack Rawfolds Mill during the disturbances of 1812. The general explanation for this 'Dumb Steeple' was that it was built to mark the boundary of Kirklees Park. If we try to probe the meaning of the word "dumb" we discover that besides its more obvious meanings, it also is a variant of the word "dummy" or "sham" - the well known folly builder's expression! So we have a "sham steeple" - simple enough! There is however, one further possibility. The same dictionary informs us that in

American parlance, a "dummy" is a person who stakes a claim for land on another's behalf. This ties in with the alleged purpose of the Mirfield "Steeple", so all things considered it seems likely that the Dumb Steeple at Grange Moor was built to mark the boundary of the Whitley Beaumont estates. Perhaps the steeple had some hidden family significance for the Beaumonts, which prompted Squire Richard to rebuild it. We can but speculate.

Here, by Squire Beaumont's Steeple, an oddity of the past stands dwarfed by an oddity of the present, the Emley Moor Transmitter, which dominates the near horizon. It towers over the landscape, and summons us to kneel in its awesome presence. *Pass through the houses to Denby Lane. Turn right down Denby Lane then right again down Ben Booth Lane, passing Ben Booth Cottage on right with views back to Dumb Steeple.*

On reaching the busy A642 Wakefield Road turn left a short distance, passing Old Hall Farm on the right. Before reaching houses and farm buildings, turn right down a grassy track between new fencing and tree planting (the site of a former mine). Before reaching the end of the track turn right through a stile, following an overgrown path between fences which winds around a reclaimed area before descending to a stile beyond a gully. From here the path leads down the side of arable fields to Flockton, passing the Zion Independent Chapel on the right, which stands aloof from the village in the fields. Built in 1802 this Georgian building has a fine five bay front and two symmetrically placed entrances.

From Flockton we head for Emley Moor. On reaching the A637 turn left into the village. Ignore Haigh Lane leading off towards Emley Moor and continue onwards passing farms and houses. Just beyond Crooked Croft on the right, and a black nissen type hut on the left, turn right down the side of new housing, descending over broken ground to a stone bridge over a stream. Pass the front of the cottage and follow the farm road past a further cottage to a T-junction of farm roads. Turn left and a short distance on, by a tiny dutch barn, turn right up a grassy track between hedgerows. On reaching a stile bear diagonally right up the field to two stiles on the skyline. Bear right, skirting around the back of farm buildings to join a farm track leading past The Mouse House. At a junction bear left, then just beyond Crawshaw Cottage turn right up Stringer House Lane.

Entering the main road to the west of Emley, the scent of coal fires and sooty chimneypots is carried on the wind. Turn right, passing Springfield

Terrace and Westfield Lane. Continue onwards along Jagger Lane to the viewing area beneath the Emley Moor TV Transmitter.

The Emley Moor Transmitter is not open to the public, but if it was it would undoubtedly make a fortune. Its scale is such, that as you plod over the fields towards it, it never seems to get any nearer. You walk, and walk, and then, just as you are beginning to feel that you are never going to get there, it suddenly towers over your head, and you crane your neck back in awe! The transmitter is owned by the Independent Broadcasting Authority. The traditional BBC presence in the area, the Holme Moss Transmitter is, weather permitting, visible to the west, a tall mast on the inhospitable moorlands around Black Hill. In actuality though, there is no inter channel rivalry, as along with YTV and Channel 4, the Emley Moor Transmitter also puts out BBCs 1 and 2.

Like its western neighbour, the Emley Moor Transmitter was also a mere mast until its sudden collapse in a storm on 15th May 1969, when it partially destroyed a chapel. Consequently it was decided that the new transmitter should be a curved and tapered concrete tower, topped by a steel aerial support mast. Such was the scale of this undertaking that the concrete foundations had to be built down to the sandstone bedrock 20 feet below ground level in order to take the weight of the tower. Work had begun by August 1969 and was completed by November 1970. By 21st January 1971, the transmitter was on the air once more.

The transmitter's vital statistics are impressive to say the least. The concrete tower itself is 900 feet high, and the Microwave Link Room and 184 foot aerial mast on top of that pushes the total height up to 1084 feet, which outstrips Blackpool Tower by 516 feet ! The ascent of the tower by lift takes 7 minutes. The 80 foot diameter of the concrete shell at the base tapers to $21^{1}/_{4}$ feet at the top. The initial thickness of the shell is 21 inches, which gradually thins to a top thickness of $13^{1}/_{2}$ inches. The tower weighs 11,200 tonnes, the foundations alone weighing 5,400 of them.

The designers of the tower were Ove Arup and Partners, the contractors Tileman & Co Ltd., and one wonders if in future times, their names will echo down the halls of history with those of Henry Flitcroft, John Edward Wainhouse, William Aislabie and John Carr (folly builders all!). We can but wait and see!

From Emley Moor continue onwards to the junction with Common Lane, just beyond which a signed track leads off right, passing a rugby field on the left. Follow this farm road to Moor Top Lane.Turn left along Moor Top Lane, passing the junction with Long Lane on the right. Continue onwards, passing the Dartmouth Arms, just beyond which a path leads off left towards Lepton, passing over a fascinating area of old mines and scrubland, pockmarked by the spoil of early "bell ground" coal mining activity. Hereabouts the flora seems more reminiscent of North Cornwall than West Yorkshire! Beyond we skirt playing fields, a cricket ground and the Highlanders Sports and Social Club before joining the busy A642.

Turn right onto the main road, passing the White Horse before turning left down a farm track passing between trees. Pass across the front of cottages then follow the footpath to the right, down the side of a wall before joining another farm road beyond a derelict cottage. At a junction bear right, following a track into woodland (ignore track leading off right).

Beyond a small house by a stream, the path ascends through coniferous forest to a junction of metalled roads. Continue onwards towards Whitley Moor, passing through a stile on the right to a second fence stile at the top of the escarpment edge. Turn left to the gaunt ruin of the Whitley Moor Gazebo.

Leastways that's what the guidebooks call it. Two locals I met referred to it as "t'divvle's tower"! If you were to visit this desolate structure on a dark wild day, it would not be hard to find reasons for the epithet. There is something creepy about the Whitley Moor Gazebo, where the raw wind howls through crumbling stones and sightless windows, framed in a soulless web of electricity pylons. Less dramatically, other sources refer to the folly as the "Temple" or "The Summer House". Here are gentler connotations!

Like the Dumb Steeple the Gazebo is associated with the Whitley-Beaumont Estate. According to tradition there is reputedly a secret passage which leads here from Whitley Hall. Another legend says that when "Black Dick" Beaumont was born in 1574, a cask of wine was hidden in the tunnel to be opened on his 21st Birthday. Secret passages smacks of priest holes, and the sixteenth century persecution of Catholic recusants, but I'm afraid I'm going to have to disappoint the romantics: the gazebo was built around 1740, as its distinctively neo-classical architecture testifies.

The most striking architectural feature of the gazebo is the fact that it once had a deep, brick lined basement. The original floor of the summer house has gone, and the entrance door leads straight onto an eight foot drop, to piles of rubble below. This was almost certainly a wine cellar, access to it being through a door in the foundations. During the miner's strike of 1926, this basement was apparently used as a "day hole". Being already set deep into the ground, it would have been a simple matter to take up its floor and dig out the coal seam beneath. What this must have done to the foundations of the gazebo doesn't bear thinking about. The existence of the "passage to Whitley Hall" legend is undoubtedly due to the presence of this mysterious basement/"dayhole".

It is said you can see York Minster from the Gazebo. Certainly you can see everything else. The Jubilee Tower on Castle Hill stands opposite, and there are fine views to the High Pennines with Holme Moss towering over the Huddersfield Valleys, close by the Derbyshire/Cheshire border. To the north-west, the South Pennine Moors around Hebden Bridge are visible, with a distant Stoodley Pike, and nearer at hand are the hills around Halifax, with the Wainhouse Tower poking up from the slopes of the Calder Valley. A distant white speck in the midst of the moors beyond Halifax marks the Withens Hotel, which, since the boundary re-organisation thrust the Tan Hill Inn into the neighbouring county, has claimed the title of "Yorkshire's Highest Inn". The hilltop settlement to the right of it, which towers over the Calderdale moors, is Queensbury, high above Bradford, and the adjacent cone of trees with the small radio mast marks the summit of Horton Bank Top, Bradford's "Reevy Beacon".

To the north-east, the Dales are just in view with the moors around Almscliff Crag and Washburndale clearly visible. To the east lies the urban sprawl of the Heavy Woollen District around Dewsbury and beyond, the rolling urban landscapes of Greater Leeds. South east, and the view simply disappears into the cooling tower generated haze of lowland Yorkshire. To the South is Emley Moor.

The walk back to Grange Moor is interesting and pleasant enough, if confusing. From the folly follow the path to the road and turn right. A short distance on, turn left down a track. Just before reaching a metalled road, a signed path leads over fields, passing pylons. Following signs, bear right, then left, with a stream on the right, to reach the road just beyond a farm.

Turn right, then right again, down the side of Pendle Hill Grange. A stile, followed by a deterring climb over a fence gives access to a path which leads along the left side of a wooded gully. The path runs along a steep contour, and boggy ground and holly bushes force diversion. Beyond a fence and stile bear left up open pasture following an indistinct path to a stile and gate. Beyond two more stiles, a wooded gully is crossed by a small pond, and a path leads past Freedom House to a stile. Cross the road to Grange Moor Post Office, and proceed up Bedford Avenue. Turn right to the start of the walk.

A whole range of countryside between here and the venerable village of Thornhill is worthy of exploration, but by now you will be thinking of rest for aching limbs, so you will be uninclined to wander further. If, when you have relaxed and refreshed yourself, you still have a thirst for exploration, the Yorkshire Mining Museum is just down the road. Here you can make up for not being allowed up Emley Moor by descending a mine shaft which is as deep as Blackpool Tower is high. The guide there, Geoff, is an old friend of mine, who, when not guiding you around the maze of underground "main gates" and "tail gates", and drawing on his long experience as a miner, follows country music with sixguns and stetson! The museum puts the mining history of the area into a very real perspective. If you've ever wondered how coal was (and is) won, at Caphouse you will find the answer.

The upland area between Huddersfield, Denby Dale, Dewsbury and Wakefield has long been an off-the-beaten-track region, a semi rural backwater of upland pastures, red brick hamlets, spoil heaps and collieries. Hardly a place to attract ramblers you might say. Could it be we are about to witness a change? Already the Kirklees Way comes through this area, and the maps betray a multiplicity of footpaths leading through woodland, hill and dale. The scope for the walker in this fine upland area has yet to be fully exploited. The purist in me hopes that it will be spared the mushrooming of waymarks, footpath signs, interpretive centres, and similar.

3: THE EARL CRAG MONUMENTS

On this walk we visit a stone pinnacle, indulge in a bracing promenade along crags, and ascend a fine prospect tower with extensive views of Upper Airedale. We then visit a mysterious moorland boulder with a strange legend attached to it.

Getting there:	Follow the A629 from Keighley towards Skipton (NOT the Aire Valley Trunk Road). At Crosshills bear left following the A6068 Colne Road through Glusburn to Cowling. Just beyond Cowling turn left up Old Lane which beyond a sharp bend becomes Piper Lane. This leads past Far Place (on the right) to Stake Hill. Park in a rough car park beside the road, from which an obvious path leads down the wallside to Wainman's Pinnacle.
Distance:	2¹/₂ miles Easy. Little more than a stroll.
Map ref:	SD 986 426 Landranger 103, or Pathfinder 670 Barnoldswick & Earby
Rating:	Walk * Follies and General Interest ***

This is the simplest and easiest walk in the book, yet what it lacks in distance it more than makes up for in interest. With two fine follies, magnificent views, and ample scope for a picnic or an exciting rock scramble, Earl Crag is a jumble of gritstone rocks with numerous fissures and small caves which invite exploration.

The Earl Crag Monuments have long held for me a special fascination. Unwittingly, at the tender age of seven or eight, I was brought here by my uncle, who sat proudly at the wheel of "Bluey", his recently acquired Morris 8. In those days owning a car (any car!) was a luxury, and a run out in Uncle Bill's car, even with the regular breakdowns, was a treat indeed! We parked up on the roadside, visited the tower (timidly ascending the dark staircase) and then explored the crags, where we picnicked and scrambled amongst the boulders. We picked some heather, decked out Bluey's radiator

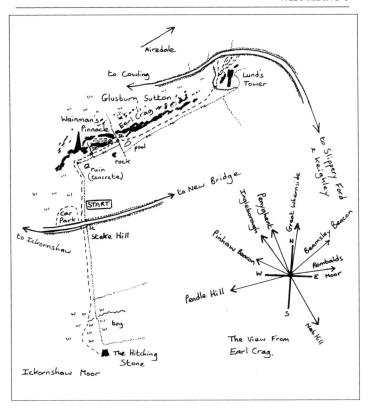

The View From Earl Crag.

with a sprig, and then headed for home, stopping for a paddle in Keighley Tarn en route. This was my first visit to the Earl Crag Monuments and I have been in love with them ever since!

Like all follies the Earl Crag Monuments have their share of mystique. No one really seems to know what to call them. My Uncle Bill referred to them as "Cowling Pinnacles". Other people confuse the names - is it Wainman's Tower and Lund's Pinnacle? or Wainman's Pinnacle and Lund's Tower. Here, now and for the record be it known that the Tower is Lund's and the Pinnacle is Wainman's!!

Park by the road at Stake Hill, where an obvious route leads down the wallside to Wainman's Pinnacle. The pinnacle stands at a junction of paths on a natural boulder on the edge of Earl Crag, overlooking Carr Head. The view from the pinnacle comes as something of a surprise, as the magnificent prospect across the valley opens up suddenly and quite unexpectedly.

In true folly fashion, not much is known about Wainman's Pinnacle. As a result it has become the object of much fanciful yarn spinning. According to one account it was erected by Lady Amcotts, the young wife of one of the Wainmans. She, so the story goes, erected the pinnacle in memory of her much lamented husband who had died fighting for the royalist cause in the Civil Wars. Another account suggests that the pinnacle was erected in 1815 to commemorate Wellington's defeat of Napoleon at the Battle of Waterloo, and that, for my money, is the more likely reason for its construction. One thing we know for sure, is that by the end of the

Lund's Tower, Earl Crag

nineteenth century the pinnacle had been severely damaged by lightning, being subsequently demolished and rebuilt in January 1900 by Messrs Gott and Riddiough of Cowling. This is the pinnacle which we see today.

From Wainman's Pinnacle turn right, following a path which is basically a high level promenade along the grim, black rock rampart of Earl Crag, with fine views across Airedale to Rombald's Moor. After a succession of stiles we proceed over a pleasant grassy sward to Lund's Tower, with its internal staircase.

Lund's Tower is a thrill for the kids. Unlike most prospect towers it is actually accessible, with a winding newel staircase leading up through semi darkness to a small turret, from which imaginary boiling oil can be poured over onto imaginary assailants! More confusion - the tower is sometimes known as "Sutton Pinnacle"! Again reliable facts are hard to come by. It is generally accepted that the tower was built at the instigation of Mr James Lund of Malsis Hall, but no-one really seems to know why. Was it built to commemorate the 21st Birthday of his daughter Ethel, or was it built to mourn her death? Another story says it was built to celebrate Queen Victoria's Jubilee, but doesn't say which one! The Earl Crag follies hold their secrets well.

From Lund's Tower we retrace our steps back along the crags to Wainman's Pinnacle, behind which the brooding whaleback of Pendle is usually in view. From here we proceed back to the car - but this is not the end of our perambulation!

Now in the opposite direction, for the third curiosity of our walk, which is reached by proceeding up the wallside towards Ickornshaw Moor. Where the wall turns off left at the edge of open moor, we encounter a massive boulder. This is the Hitching Stone.

The Hitching Stone cannot speak. One feels that if it could it would tell us a fine story, but it stands alone and forlorn, muted by the chill wind which sighs through the heather of Ickornshaw Moor. On a wet and murky day this lonely place seems eerie, quite untouched by the hand of man, but this is not so. At one time, amazingly, a fair was held at this bleak spot. It was, apparently, an annual occurrence, being held each August by the local villagers, who had stalls, quoits, footracing, horse racing and eating treacle pudding contests! The fair was apparently a highly partisan event, the villagers of Sutton and Cowling keeping their stalls within their own boundaries! Today it is not even a living memory.

The Hitching Stone is 21 feet high, and reputedly about 1000 tons in weight. Here we are standing 1,180 feet above sea level, and the views are excellent. Beamsley Beacon, Simon's Seat, Great Whernside, Buckden Pike, Pen-y-Ghent, Ingleborough and Pendle are (weather permitting) all in view. On the near horizon lie the Maw Stones, and beyond, over the hill, the Pennine Way struggles across the soggy wildernesses between Ponden and Lothersdale, passing the Wolf Stones by the boundary fence on the summit of Ickornshaw Moor. The Hitching Stone marks the meeting point of

The Hitching Stone, Ickornshaw Moor
St. David's Ruin, Bingley

Keppel's Column, Wentworth Woodhouse

three different moors and is also the boundary between the ancient Wapentakes of Staincliff and Skyrack. There is something brooding and pagan about the stone, and, not surprisingly, there is a legend attached to it.

Long ago a "cunning woman" who lived on the edge of Rombald's Moor became increasingly dissatisfied with this huge boulder which lay in front of her cottage. Curses had no result, and in the end, livid with anger, she took a stout stick, inserted it into a hole in the rock and "hitched" it across the valley to where it now stands.

The boulder "fits" the story. High up in the side of the rock is a strange recess, known as the "Priest's Chair", and connected to this, a smooth, round hole runs right through the rock, its sides curiously patterned in parts. According to the geologists the hole was caused by the weathering out of a large fossil tree (Lepidodendron). Our unscientific ancestors however had a different explanation - this was the hole the witch used to "hitch" the stone, and the pattern was made by the wood grain of her stick! One suspects, however, that the hole was the origin of the story rather than the story the origin of the hole!!

The Hitching Stone has one surprise left. Clamber up it. You will find that its top is cloven, and contains not, as you might imagine, a platform of weathered rock but a deep bath full of clean rainwater! With the kids suitably soaked, squelch back down the moor to search for those towels you thought you'd packed in the car! If you have time (as you probably will with so short a walk) it is but a short drive over the moors to Oakworth, where there is a fine grotto in the Park, or to Keighley, where the Cliffe Castle Museum with its rocky conservatory, is both fascinating and free!!

4: SLACK, LONGWOOD EDGE AND THE NAB END TOWER

Woodlands, crags and sweeping Pennine views characterise this interesting walk on the fringes of urban Huddersfield. Its chief attractions are the site of a Roman Fort, an open air theatre and the curious Nab End Tower.

Getting there:	M62 to junction 24. Follow the A643 (Rochdale Road) to Outlane. Park just beyond the village in lay-by by the bus terminus, shop and public conveniences. A sign points to Outlane Golf Club and a lane leads under the M62. This is the start of our walk.
Distance:	5 miles approx. Easy enough, but watch the kids on Longwood Edge.
Map ref:	SE 083 177 Pathfinder 702 Huddersfield & Marsden
Rating:	Walk ** Follies and General interest **

> On Longwood Edge there stands a Tower,
> that end near Quarmby Clough,
> and if you stand out by the church,
> you'll see it plain enough.
> This Tower was built by men and boys
> of Longwood that is true,
> and if you want the height of it
> it's twenty nine feet two.
> So come my lads and lasses gay,
> come, and join the throng,
> We'll have a spree this Longwood Thump
> in eighteen sixty one.

GEORGE COLLIER

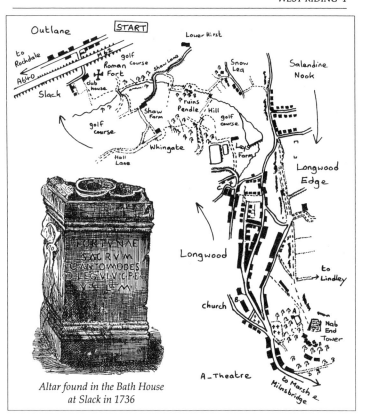

*Altar found in the Bath House
at Slack in 1736*

Outlane, a linear village straddling the A640 Rochdale Road, is a schizophrenic community. Sited on the long, high, ridge which separates the Calder Valley and its tributaries from the Colne Valley, it seems uncertain of its true identity. To say that local people are partisan is putting it mildly. On the one side of the road people read *The Examiner* and follow the fortunes of Huddersfield Town, whilst on the other side *The Halifax Courier* is taken, and people are more likely to be interested in developments at the Shay or Thrum Hall. Recently it was suggested that the M62 should become the boundary between the two adjacent local authorities -

a move which would have put Kirklees into Kirklees and Outlane into 'Calderdale'. The villagers at Outlane protested fiercely. They like the boundary where it is - running right through the village!

Our route passes under the M62 to Outlane Golf Club, which stands adjacent to the cottages at Slack, where the heavy traffic of the motorway thunders along the northern boundary of the Golf Course. Few of the people who devote their weekends to golfing here will realise that they are following in the footsteps of the Roman Legions, for on the golf course at Slack once stood a small fort, a far flung outpost of the mighty Roman Empire. No trace of the fort is visible at ground level. There is the occasional mound and the odd bank, but these earthworks are more to do with golfing than with ancient occupation. To see an outline of the fort you would need an aircraft. Even when viewed from the hillside opposite there is no visible trace.

It is generally believed that the fort at Slack was constructed around AD 79-80 by Cnaeus Julius Agricola, the Roman general and military engineer who (fortunately for posterity) was the father-in-law of the Roman historian Tacitus, who gave us the only surviving account of the Roman conquest of Britain. The fort was built to defend the transpennine section of the important Roman military road connecting the legionary headquarters at Deva (Chester) with that of Eboracum (York), which hereabouts probably followed the line of the present M62 Motorway. The bleak Agricolan fort covered nearly four acres and was constructed almost entirely of earth and timber. The corners of the fort faced the cardinal points, and the ramparts, 20 feet wide, were built of turf sods resting upon an 8 feet course of stones. The enclosed area was 356 feet square. According to an inscribed stone noted in 1757 it was built by the "Centuria of Reburrinus". All the gates of this fort were wooden, and were for the most part flanked by wooden towers. There was a paved parade ground. Later, during the reign of Trajan, much of the fort was reconstructed in stone.

To the east of the fort was a bathhouse and to the north an annexe - a small civilian settlement serving the garrison. Besides keeping an eye on the turbulent Brigantes, the settlement would also have provided "services" for weary transpennine travellers. After crossing the wild moors the little community at Slack must have been a welcome sight. If you have visited the amazingly well preserved fort at Housesteads on Hadrian's Wall, you will not find it too difficult to visualise the kind of settlement that once existed here, among the fairways and bunkers.

What did the Romans call their fort at Slack? Was it perhaps the elusive Cambodunum, that mysterious settlement mentioned in the Antonine Itinerary as lying between Calcaria (Tadcaster) and Mancunium (Manchester)? It seems likely. Certainly the Roman altar found at Greetland would suggest that it was sited hereabouts. Perhaps one day further discoveries may provide the answer.

Little is known about the fort's history. A tile of the ninth legion has been found, along with one with the name of the Fourth Cohort of the Breuci from Pannonia. Pevsner maintains that the fort was abandoned during the reign of Hadrian, and its garrison sent north to work on the Wall around AD 125. This may be true, but it is equally possible that the fort had a garrison right up to the withdrawal of Roman troops from Britain in the fifth century. There is no written history, and archaeology gives us but a fragmentary picture.

The fort was excavated in 1865, when the remains of stone buildings were found along with numerous stamped tiles. Various finds had been made in earlier times - an altar to Fortune for example, had been found in the bath house at Slack in 1736. The full excavation of the bathhouse revealed a hypocaust - a complete Roman underfloor heating system, and this was removed and re-erected in Greenhead Park, Huddersfield (I could not locate it - perhaps it has been moved again). Parts of the fort - the Commandant's House for example - were never excavated.

So, haunted by the ghosts of golfers and departed Roman legionaries we proceed on our way. From the Golf Club, turn left into the car park. Proceed to its bottom left-hand side where a path, initially screened by hedges, descends the wallside towards the beck, with the golf course on the left. The path bears left along the slope to a high bridge over the Longwood Brook. Do not cross the bridge, instead continue onwards, following a narrow (and at times precarious) path along the northern slope of Shaw Clough, descending finally to Shaw Lane Bridge. At a junction of tracks take the right-hand fork, which descends to and recrosses the beck. Ignore the waymarked path leading upwards towards the golf course; instead bear left, following a well used track which leads back over the beck through an assortment of ruined buildings before proceeding down the left-hand bank of a stream to a footbridge. This is not the right of way, but is nevertheless the way most in use. (The actual right of way is overgrown, hard to find and is not helped by the resiting of one stile and the blocking of another!)

From the footbridge turn left up the wallside to emerge into a lane by Snow Lea. Turn right and proceed along the lane until a path is encountered on the left, leading up a field to steps and quarry workings. This leads up between crags to emerge into Gilead Road. Turn right along this (passing Centuria Walk on the left) and continue to its junction with Raw Nook Road.

Ignoring the road down to Longwood, continue onwards along the track which leads onto Longwood Edge, becoming a fine high level promenade along high crags, with playing fields on the left. Proceed to the junction with Haughs Lane.

Here a choice must be made. You can continue onwards along the edge of the crags - the path is quite distinct put decidedly "airy" in parts, and must be negotiated with care - or you can descend Bull Green Road to re-ascend the edge by a track lower down. Eventually the two routes re-unite and a path leads without complication to Nab End Tower.

Words cannot describe this structure. Shapeless, buttressed, a black monstrosity capped with concrete, it stands like a giant upturned flowerpot or a Pictish broch! It is constructed of drystone masonry and is an excellent example of the craft of those forgotten artisans whose work is more usually to be found in the massive retaining walls which so characterise the quarrying areas of the West Riding. A staircase with a metal bannister rail runs around the outside of the structure to a concreted viewing platform with a central metal pipe which looks as if it was intended for a flagpole.

It comes as no surprise to discover that there are various stories explaining this decidedly weird structure. According to one version it was built to commemorate the Crimean War of 1854-1856, but the tower was built in 1860-1! According to another account it was erected to the memory of Richard Oastler, that Huddersfield land agent who was the arch foe of child labour in factories and mines. Oastler died in 1861. An even less plausible explanation suggests it was erected as a latter day beacon site. A similar tower was once sited by Linthwaite Church, and the theory is that the one gave light to the other. Unfortunately the telegraph had been invented in 1858!

The true explanation is far less romantic. The tower was erected by local working folk simply for amusement and to kill time while work was slack due to a slump in trade. It was meant to be a novelty for the Longwood "Thump" (Feast) of 1861. No architects were employed or plans made. The young men of the neighbourhood simply devoted a few summer evenings to getting stone from the disused delfs nearby, which they relayed to the site by passing the stones hand to hand along a human chain. Local neighbours provided them with money for drinks, the lads ending each evening's toil in the pub! The building of the tower was supervised by one George Hellawell, a local mason who was deaf and dumb. It is his initials and the date that are carved on a stone set into the tower. When the tower was complete the adjacent chasm was filled in, resulting in a piece of level ground capable of providing standing room for about 2000 people. A novel recreation area had been created.

An article which was printed in the *Huddersfield Examiner* on 17th August 1861 gives us some interesting insights into the origins of the tower:

A NOVEL ERECTION. The great novelty of the [Longwood] Feast has been the tower at Nab End. It is a curious affair. It stands about 20 feet high and 12 or 15 feet wide at the base. It is entirely solid throughout, being built of dry stones.... The tower has been built (under the permission of William Shaw, Esq., the proprietor of the land) by the working men of the neighbourhood. Nab Hill is much frequented during the summer and doubtless the tower will add to its interest.... the completion of the tower was celebrated in due form during the feast. The inauguration commenced on Saturday last and continued several days. A grand dinner, got up by subscription, was partaken of on the ground by upwards of a hundred working men. Fireworks were set off, and other proceedings of a festive character were liberally engaged in. Even poesy lent its aid to immortalise the occasion. Two pieces, composed expressly in honour of the wonderful tower, by Mr. Collier of Milnsbridge, and Mr. John Smith of Golcar, were recited and sung. The affair has given rise to a great deal of merriment in the neighbourhood. It is hinted that the proprietor of the land intends giving the tower a finishing touch some day, and making it into something useful in the shape of an observatory.

He never did so. By the 1880's "Rambler" was reporting in articles in the *Huddersfield Chronicle* that the tower had become dilapidated: "But the tower is not what it once was.... During the last twenty years visitors have amused themselves in throwing stones from the top, and then by degrees it has been reduced in height, till the top is only five or six yards from the ground."

Fortunately the article awoke a response to the tower's plight. Mr George Shaw, grandson of the original landowner, paid some unemployed workmen in the area to restore the tower to its former glory, and in 1895 he presented the tower and adjacent quarry to Huddersfield Corporation. The council have since added three buttresses to its western side to prevent collapse, and have capped the whole thing with concrete in an attempt to stave off the ravages of vandalism.

Of all the follies we have visited in this book, none of them have been as spontaneous in their nature as this bizarre structure. There was no plan, no final vision. Its construction was simply an event - a Victorian "happening". Stones were collected and the whole thing constructed instinctively. This singular fact must surely make the Longwood Tower unique among the architectural curiosities of Britain.

The tower is not the only structure of interest on Longwood Edge. A few yards away by the steps is an open air theatre. This was built in 1873, having been "restored" with concrete in 1930. Why was it built? It seems likely that it too, like the tower, was associated with the annual Longwood Thump. Perhaps village pageants were performed here? It would be interesting to know the answer.

Our walk passes the open air theatre and descends the steps to enter Longwood village by the War Memorial (shops, toilets, etc.). Bear right up Longwood Gate, passing the Church on the left. A short distance on, turn left down Prospect Road, passing between mills and then houses before reaching the road's dead end by a playground. Cross the recreation ground diagonally to join a descending walled ginnel by a street lamp. Descend to Grove Street (among mills) and bear right to the junction of four lanes by cottages. Turn left up Royles Head Lane, which quickly becomes Holmefield Road. Just beyond the mansion turn right onto a farm road to Leys Farm.

At Leys Farm bear left through a gate (and cow wallow!), following a path up the hillside towards trees, with the reservoir on the left. Beyond a knoll, pass through a fence stile and turn right along a path which soon leads over the golf course towards trees. On reaching trees pass through a gate to enter a walled lane leading to the ruins of Pendle House, now cleft by a neatly groomed golfer's route. Beyond, the lane bears left up the hillside through the woods. Do NOT follow it. Instead bear right, then left, following a rather less obvious path which winds up the hillside with a wall on the left. Pass over open ground to a wall stile, just beyond a tree-capped knoll. Continue onwards through a wood, contouring the hillside to another wall stile. Beyond, a field path leads around the rear of Whingate before entering the access road through a gate in the fence. Pass down the side of Whingate to join a lane descending to Shaw Farm.

At Shaw Farm turn left along the field side then right through an unusual stile, following a descending fence towards the brook. On reaching the edge of the ravine turn left through a stile (below a golfer's tee) and cross the bridge over the brook to rejoin the outward route on far side. Turn left, and follow the path back up to Outlane Golf Club and the start of our perambulation.

5: ST DAVID'S RUIN, BINGLEY

A "Mow Cop" style folly, pleasant woods, a waterfall, moors, an obelisk and Lady Blantyre's favourite rock are all to be found on this enjoyable ramble which starts by the River Aire in Bingley.

Getting there:	A650 from Bradford to Bingley. Park (if possible!) outside Myrtle Park (Start of the walk). Alternative parking available in a massive car park by station and canal (pay and display).
Distance:	9 miles. You can take the kids but they will be tired. The walk passes through two public parks - Myrtle Park and St Ives.
Map ref:	SE 107 389 Landranger 104
Rating:	Walk *** Follies and General Interest **

Bingley is pleasant little town in the Aire Valley twixt Bradford and Keighley. Famous for its Five Rise Locks, fine old church, Damart long johns and leaning chimney, Bingley straddles the bustling A650, horrendously busy of late since it became the bottleneck for the unfinished (and controversial) Aire Valley Trunk Road, which now pours its rush hour traffic into the old road at nearby Crossflatts.

St. David's Ruin.

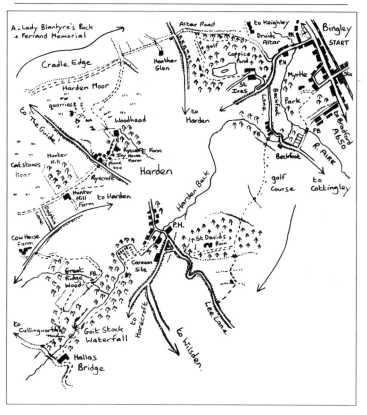

Our walk begins by the bandstand in Myrtle Park. Nearby is the town hall, which was formerly "Myrtle Grove", a mansion built by Johnson Atkinson Busfield in 1772. It was described by Wesley as a "little Paradise", and from it our walk leads through the park to a footbridge which passes over an island in the river, passing allotments to enter Beckfoot Lane. At Beckfoot, near the confluence of the Harden Beck with the River Aire there is a fine old packhorse bridge and adjacent ford standing near a farmhouse dated 1617. On the gable ends are stone lanterns which denote the one time manorial rights of the Knights of St John - the Hospitallers.

120 yards beyond Beckfoot Bridge turn left over a smaller footbridge

from which an indistinct path leads up over the golf course following a line of whitewashed boulders. Beyond a stile, bear left uphill round to a small gate which gives access to a coniferous plantation (Ruin Bank Wood). The path ascends steeply through the wood, where hides St David's Ruin, unfortunately situated on private land.

St David's Ruin was built as an eyecatcher to St Ives across the valley by Benjamin Ferrand in 1796. It provided the inspiration for John Braine's fictional "St Clair Folly" in *Room at the Top*. It consists basically of a contrivedly ruined circular tower with a high Gothic arch attached to it. It is typical of a type of folly, the best example of which may be found at Mow Cop, Staffordshire. Not too long ago it could be viewed easily from a distance, but now it is lost in coniferous forest.

From the stile at the edge of wood, proceed diagonally across the field, the next field, and then alongside a wall into Lee Lane. Turn right and proceed down to the Malt Shovel Inn at Harden Beck (which features in Willliam Riley's Way of The Winepress).

Cross the bridge, then turn left onto the metalled road which leads up to the caravan site in Goit Stock Woods. Beyond the site, follow a rocky path up the wooded gorge to Goit Stock Waterfall, a charming spot, although the waters of the beck are somewhat polluted - a sad fate for such an attractive watercourse. Ascend alongside the falls and follow the path to Hallas Bridge.

Cross Hallas Bridge, and ignoring the main track up to Cullingworth, turn right, following a footpath through the wood to a stile, which returns to woodland again after crossing a small pasture. Beyond the woods, follow the track down to a footbridge over a small stream then ascend to a gate and stile in the wall. Turn left and follow a footpath which enters the Cullingworth Road by a bus stop. Cross the road and turn right, following the road 200 yards before turning left up Dolphin Lane, which leads up to Catstones Moor. At the top of the lane turn right and follow the well defined path to the road and phone box at Ryecroft.

Cross the road and follow a track round through farms to a bungalow alongside a ravine. Beyond, a path leads onto Harden Moor, soon becoming lost in a maze of paths and extensive quarry workings. Follow an old, paved (and partially overgrown) quarry road which leads right over the moor to join the track from the Guide Inn. At a junction of ways, continue onwards for a few yards before turning right through a stile into a pasture. Follow a path alongside the wall through a succession of stiles (one tight!) until a track is joined from Heather Glen. Continue along this track to the Harden-Keighley Road.

Cross the road and proceed onwards down the Altar Road, with the boundary wall of St Ives Golf Course on the right. Soon a high ladder stile appears in the wall. Climb over and follow the well defined track which leads across the golf course then alongside a wall with seats, heather and birch trees. At a junction of paths take the right fork to the Ferrand Memorial and Lady Blantyre's Rock.

The Ferrand Obelisk is something of a disappointment. The marble memorial seems somehow out of place in this landscape of heather and boulders. It is functional and about as un-eccentric as you can get. The inscription (which runs all round its faces) explains all:

> In Bingley Cemetery rests Wm. Ferrand of St Ives who so affectionately dedicated the rustic monument below this rock to my dear mother and I. Fanny Mary Ferrand, his loving wife

The Ferrand Obelisk

dedicate this memorial to his dear and lamented memory.

In early life he took an active part in support of the Ten Hours Factory Bill and after 17 years of ceaseless effort he assisted as M.P. for Knaresborough in carrying it through the House of Commons.

He brought under notice the iniquities of the truck system and a stringent law was passed to compel the payment of wages in the current coin of the realm, He vigorously exposed the harsh clauses of the new Poor Law, until they were removed from the statute book and he was the firm denouncer of all corruption among public men. He planted about 400 acres of wood for the benefit of the property and to beautify his native place.

He was MP for Knaresborough from 1841 to 1847, and for Devonport from 1863 to 1865. He was a Deputy Lieutenant of the West Riding and acted as a magistrate for nearly 50 years, during a great proportion of which time he presided as chairman of the Keighley petty sessional division in perfect harmony with his fellow magistrates.

He died 31st March 1889 in his 80th year.

The "rustic monument" to which the inscription refers is Lady Blantyre's Rock which is a much more appropriate monument than the obelisk which refers to it. A large natural boulder with a sheltered overhang has the inscribed stone beneath which once again obligingly explains all: "The Dowager Lady Blantyre for nearly 30 years was accustomed in summer to sit under this rock reading and enjoying the scenery.

In 1857 St Ives was altered and enlarged from plans entirely drawn by herself and her daughter the Hon Mrs Ferrand. The Terrace and its flower garden were also designed by them.

Her Ladyship ended her last visit on the 21st November 1874, and died resting on the Rock of Ages at Lennoxlove in East Lothian on the 19th of the following November in her 84th year, with faculties unimpaired, and most deeply lamented.

Mr Ferrand, her son-in-law, mournfully designated this rustic monument to her beloved memory, and with confidence requests the future owner to preserve it as an affectionate memento of "the best of mothers and the sweetest of Women."

From Lady Blantyre's Rock our route proceeds past Coppice Pond to the mansion of St Ives, now the headquarters of the Sports Turf Research Institute, which deals with golf courses in Guinea and bowling greens in Buenos Aires! The St Ives Estate has a cafe, toilets, nature trails, playground and a golf club.

Proceed down the St Ives carriageway, cross the Harden/Bingley road, and continue along Beckfoot Lane to rejoin the outward route near Beckfoot Bridge. From here we simply retrace our steps back across the Aire to the start of the walk in Myrtle Park. Energetic types might now consider exploring the staircase locks on the Leeds & Liverpool Canal. Most people though will be simply glad to put their feet up!

6: STOODLEY PIKE MONUMENT

Coiners, Methodists and textile magnates, mill towns, sombre moors and lonely packhorse ways are all encountered in this fine upland walk which visits Stoodley Pike Monument: lone sentinel of the Upper Calder Valley.

Getting there:	The walk starts and ends in Mytholmroyd near Hebden Bridge, West Yorkshire. The village can be reached by rail from Leeds, Bradford, Halifax, Rochdale and Manchester. It is also served by buses from Halifax, Rochdale and Burnley. Mytholmroyd stands on the busy A 646 Burnley Road, about a mile east of Hebden Bridge. Car parking is available by the County Bridge, the Burnley Road, and the Mytholmroyd Community Centre.
Distance:	8 miles. A stiff hike!
Map ref:	SE 013 258 Outdoor Leisure Sheet 21
Rating:	Walk *** General Interest ***

There are many routes up Stoodley Pike. Most commonly the ascent is tackled from Mankinholes, or Hebden Bridge. The "royal road" to Stoodley Pike is undoubtedly from Todmorden, following the "Fielden Trail" from Gaddings Reservoirs, where from start to finish the Monument will dominate your view. On this route starting from Mytholmroyd however, the Pike is not visible, and indeed will not be in view until we have walked some distance, but there are other compensations as we shall see.

The Mytholmroyd we see today was created by the industrial revolution. Being little more than a river crossing for packhorses near a few outlying farmsteads on the valley floor, the arrival of the turnpike in the eighteenth century closely followed by the Rochdale Canal (and eventually the railway) transformed this sleepy little place into a thriving industrial community. Smaller than a town, yet larger than your average village, Mytholmroyd squats on a wide

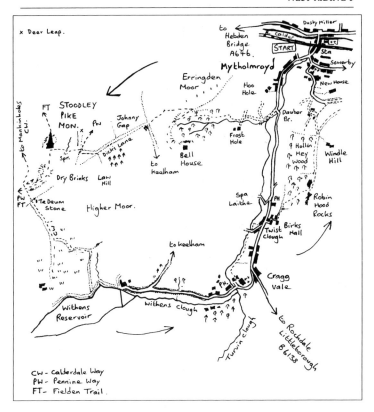

x Deer Leap.

to Hebden Bridge A646.

Dusty Miller
R. Calder
START
Sta
Sowerby
New House

Mytholmroyd

Erringden Moor

Hoo Hole

Dauber Br.

FT
STOODLEY PIKE MON.
PW
Johnny Gap
Dicks Lane
spr.

Frost Hole

Bell House

Hollin Hey Wood
Windle Hill

to Mankinholes CW.

to keelham

Dry Brinks
Law Hill

PW
FT
Te Deum Stone
Higher Moor.

Spa Laithe
PW
Robin Hood Rocks

to keelham

Twist Clough
Birks Hall

Withens Reservoir

Withens clough

PW

Cragg Vale

Turvin clough

to Rochdale Littleborough B6138

CW - Calderdale Way
PW - Pennine Way
FT - Fielden Trail.

valley floor, not so hemmed in by the hills as nearby Hebden Bridge, its precipice-girt neighbour further up the dale.

Textiles are the tenor of Mytholmroyd's more recent history. Fieldens had a cotton mill here, and the late nineteenth century saw the blossoming of a thriving blanket making industry. Fustians, corduroys and riding clothes are still made here, and in 1906 a strike in that industry led a local unemployed weaver to build a chicken hatchery in some old orange boxes. By 1906 chick sales had reached 2 million a year, and today the business (Thornber's) is one of the foremost poultry breeders in the world.

Mytholmroyd also has a niche in the annals of literature, for on Aspinall Street was born Poet Laureate Ted Hughes, who drew early inspiration from the crags of Mytholmroyd's shadowy brooding Scout, which dominates the southern side of the valley.

The village stands at the junction of two valleys, and also on the boundaries of four ancient townships (Wadsworth, Erringden, Sowerby and Midgley). Turvin Clough, running down from the moorland fastnesses of Cragg Vale pours into the heavily polluted Calder by County Bridge. This charming little rill is known locally as the Elphin Brook (further upstream it is the Cragg Brook). The same place name element is to be found at nearby Elphaborough Hall. Elphaborough translates roughly as "mound of the elves", and it could be that this place was once an abode of "the little people", those small, dark and shadowy "aboriginals" who inhabited Britain even before the Celts, and who almost certainly holed up in remote spots right down into the Middle Ages, their strange racial type and alien dialect setting them apart from later waves of people, who came to equate them with elves, little people and fairy folk.

Hollinshed's *Chronicle* of 1577 gives us our first reference to Mytholmroyd Bridge, describing the Calder as receiving "one rill near Elphabrught Bridge". This early bridge was wooden, replacing a ford here dating back to the early Middle Ages. Elphaborough Hall was once the residence of the Steward of the Earl Warren's deer park of Erringden, and in the eighteenth century it was the residence of the notorious Isaac Hartley, known as the "Duke of York" and brother to the even more notorious "King David" the self appointed leader of the Cragg Vale coiners.

The Cragg Road from Mytholmroyd Bridge leads over the moors to Blackstone Edge, with a branch road (Scout Road) to Sowerby on the outskirts of the village, yet neither of these roads were the raison d'être for the bridge itself. Prior to the arrival of the turnpike age, Mytholmroyd was but an isolated crossing place for a rugged packhorse trod, which, having crossed the river, climbed steeply up Hall Bank and out over the moors to Sowerby, from whence it led to Norland and eventually Huddersfield. All the other roads passing through Mytholmroyd are the product of a later age.

So to the walk! Our route leads out of Mytholmroyd along the Cragg Road, passing Hoo Hole on the right, where, on Thurs 28th June 1770 John

Wesley "rode to Mr. Sutcliffe's at Hoo Hole, a lovely valley encompassed with high mountains. I stood on the smooth grass before his house which stands on gently rising ground, and all the people on the slope before me. It was a glorious opportunity. I trust they 'came boldly to the throne' and found grace to help in time of need".

At Dauber Bridge turn right, following a track signed Frost Hole. Follow this track up through woodlands ignoring an uphill fork on the right. Beyond a cattle-grid where the track bears left to Frost Hole, (which, after years of dereliction is being rebuilt). Continue onwards, following a paved "causey" through the woodlands of the Broadhead Clough Nature Reserve. The Reserve belongs to the Yorkshire Naturalists Trust and is rich in birch/oak woodlands and associated wildlife. It contains large areas of sphagnum bog. The path ascends steps to the right then runs to the left below crags, before finally meeting the boundary fence. Here the path ascends steeply to the right, climbing out of Bell Hole onto the shoulder of Erringden Moor. Above Bell Hole stands Bell House Farm, perched on its crag, a lone sentinel over the valleys below.

Bell House was the residence of "King David" Hartley, and many romantic tales have been told about his gang of homespun criminals who lurked in the wild fastnesses of Cragg Vale in the latter part of the eighteenth century. More recent accounts tend to play down the romance, depicting the coiners as a bunch of hard, callous and unscrupulous rogues. To me, none of these accounts ring strictly true. Of romance, of course, there was none, such ideas come from the Robin Hood mentality of earlier generations. As for their viciousness and hardness, well the story does contain murder most foul and dark intrigue, but these things were more the consequence of a fateful chain of events rather than the consistently wicked behaviour of totally evil men. The real "evil genius" of the piece was not "King David" but an infinitely more unyielding and universal presence, that of endless, unrelenting and grinding poverty.

Poverty was a cruel master. Life was harsh for the Pennine hillfarmer of the eighteenth century. The cold, wet upland climate did not support much in the way of arable farming, so the hillfarmer had to rely largely on animal husbandry, supplementing his meagre lifestyle with the production and sale of cloth "pieces". In eighteenth-century Calderdale almost every building echoed to the "clack" of the loom and the hillsides were festooned with cloth "pieces" drying on tenter frames. An old poem gives a good picture:

> Farms with scanty crops and stacks,
> handicraft in wool and flax,
> Strings of horses carrying packs
> coiners haunting woods and slacks
> havercake lads and paddy whacks
> Such of old was Halifax!

It was to this remote, poverty stricken landscape that David Hartley returned, some time in the middle of the eighteenth century, with the intention of putting down roots and practising the new "trade" which he had picked up whilst apprenticed to an ironworker in Birmingham. He chose his house well. Bell House on its crags is sited like a fortress. Anyone approaching would be spotted long before they arrived, allowing time for any incriminating artefacts to be safely disposed of.

To practice his "business" in a profitable manner, it was necessary for "King David" to set up some sort of local organisation, so he called his friends and relatives together, and, in the style of a true "Mafioso" made them an offer which they couldn't refuse: a simple way to make easy money (quite literally)!

In the eighteenth century, because of a universal shortage of currency, all manner of unusual coins were in circulation. Portuguese Moidores, Pieces of Eight and Spanish "Pistoles" for example, were, along with other foreign currencies, accepted unquestioningly as legal tender. Coins in those days of course were made of gold and silver, not of base metal as they are today; so what was actually stamped upon the face of the coin tended to be of rather secondary importance. This made life easy for the likes of David Hartley.

The idea was brilliantly simple. Having procured a supply of golden guineas the coiners clipped off the edges, filed on new ones and returned the coins to their owners for circulation. The clippings were carefully collected and then melted down to make bogus Moidores. These passed for 27/- each, even though the coiners only put 22 shillings worth of gold into them. On seven guineas they would make about a £1 profit, which was a considerable sum in those far off days. The idea quickly caught on with the hard bitten and impoverished local population, who, thrilled by the promise of 'easy money' set to work with a will. In a very short time "King David" found himself at the centre of an ever expanding criminal empire which was even to enjoy the collusion of some local worthies and the Halifax Deputy Constable!

The fact that coining was illegal did not seem to occur to these rough hill farmers. Under the law, diminishing the currency was a "Misprision of Treason", and as such carried the death penalty. Safely ensconced in their remote farmsteads, far beyond the reach of what little law there was, they no doubt felt secure enough to carry on their trade without molestation, and for a while they did just that. Yet they were not hardened criminals. They were poor and it was easy money - It never occurred to them that debasing the currency might be to the detriment of everyone, and might even prove a threat to the national economy.

When in 1767 the Merchants of Halifax complained to the government about the debased coinage, William Dighton, the local excise man, decided to take action. Encouraged by Robert Parker, an energetic Halifax solicitor, Dighton sought to find someone who would inform on the gang, and in August 1769 near Todmorden he found his man. James Broadbent, a 33-year-old soldier turned charcoal burner who lodged at the house of Martha Eagland of Hall Gate Mytholmroyd, agreed to work for Dighton. Other informers followed.

After an abortive attempt to capture one of the coiners (Thomas Clayton) at Stannery End, the gang were alerted to the danger and £100 was offered to anyone who would dispose of Dighton for them. Shortly afterwards, the arrest of "King David" in the tap room at the Old Cock in Halifax in October 1769, and his subsequent incarceration in York Castle brought matters to a head, and a now determined Isaac Hartley hired two hit men - Robert Thomas of Wadsworth Banks and Matthew Normanton of Stannery End - to sort out Dighton once and for all. On the night of 10th November 1769 they repaired to Halifax, where they lay in wait for Dighton outside his house at Bull Green Close (now Savile Close). As he returned home just after midnight Thomas and Normanton waylaid him and shot him through the head. After kicking his body and rifling his pockets, they left his body in the street to be found by his horrified wife, who had been roused by the disturbance.

By murdering Dighton the coiners had gone too far. The country was appalled by the deed, and as Dighton was laid to rest in Halifax Parish Church, mourned by his wife and eight children, plans were already afoot to deal with the coiners. Lord Weymouth, who was a sort of eighteenth-century Home Secretary wrote to the Marquis of Rockingham about the affair, who, as Lord Lieutenant of the West Riding, decided he would come to Halifax to discuss the matter. Lord Rockingham was a former Whig Prime Minister and was destined to lead the government in 1782. He was the patron and friend of the great Edmund Burke and lived on his great estates at Wentworth Woodhouse near Rotherham (see Walk 9). The ringers of the Halifax Parish Church were paid 36/- for the visit of the Marquis, more than the fee for great naval victories. Rockingham must have been a popular man in Halifax. The Marquis made his report and left. He asked that a solicitor from the Mint be appointed to deal with the case, and by the end of 1769 a Mr William Chamberlayne had come up to Halifax to proceed against the coiners at the government's expense. On 26th December 1769 Joseph Hanson, the Deputy Constable of Halifax was charged with clipping, and escaped from custody on Christmas Eve. A price was put on his head. Other arrests followed. A £100 reward had been offered by the government for information leading to the apprehension of Dighton's murderers, followed by a further £100 from the merchants of Halifax. This led Broadbent to incriminate Thomas, Normanton and a man named Folds, who were all sent to York Castle.

At the Spring Assizes of 1770 David Hartley was sentenced to death along with James Oldfield and William Varley, and on the 28th April he was hanged on Knavesmire, his body being brought home for burial in Heptonstall churchyard. The parish registers of St Thomas à Becket, Heptonstall, contain the following entry: "1770. May I. David Hartley de Bellhouse in Villa Erringdinensis suspensus in collo prope Eboracum ob nummos publicos illicite cudendos et accidentos." (David Hartley of Bellhouse was hanged near York for unlawfully stamping and clipping public coin.)

24 other coiners (including Thomas and Normanton) who had appeared at the Spring Assizes of 1770 had their trials postponed, and were actually released on bail At the next Assizes, Broadbent's

evidence was proven to be untrustworthy. He said he had witnessed the murder of Dighton, but his self contradiction proved he had not. Thomas and Normanton were acquitted, and went home, no doubt congratulating themselves on their close shave!

With the execution of "King David" and the wave of accusations and arrests the coiners were broken. Influential persons who had secretly colluded with the coiners now condemned them openly. Bell House was left alone with its memories. For others, however, the reckoning was yet to come.

Leaving Bell Hole we plod over Erringden Moor, passing boundary stones, before arriving at the start of Dick's Lane by the ruin at Johnny Gap. In the 1840s this unlikely spot was the scene of an annual stock fair held by local farm tenants. Today, Johnny Gap is frequented only by sheep and the occasional walker.

From Johnny Gap, pass through the gate and follow Dick's Lane towards the Pike. At the end of Dick's Lane turn right, following a wall over some marshy ground to meet the Pennine Way coming in from the right. Here is the western boundary of what once was the Erringden Deer Park. Beyond is Langfield Common, which stretches along the ridge towards Todmorden.

The Pennine Way proceeds to the Public Slake Trough at Stoodley Spring, where, after a refreshing and well earned drink we head up the moor to the Pike itself.

Stoodley Pike Monument is dark, sullen and faintly Egyptian. On a sunny day it is distinguished and grey, but mostly it is moody and black. The wind howls unrelentingly up its winding staircase and whips viciously around its exposed viewing platform. On a winter's day it chills to the bone. Some shelter may be obtained between its great buttresses, but this pallid delight tends to be marred by the annoyingly humanised sheep who mug you for your sandwiches!

The present monument is the third (or possibly fourth) to be erected on this prominent site. The first monument, a cairn of stones, was erected long ago, the last resting place of some ancient chieftain. His bones were reputedly discovered by workmen digging out the foundations for the first Pike in 1814. It has been suggested that the Pike once held a beacon, (certainly one was fired here for the 1988 Armada Celebrations). At 1,310 feet above sea level, it would

Jim Jarratt
1989.

Stoodley Pike
Monument

have made an ideal site. According to some sources, a building had been erected here before 1814, but whatever this might have been it was almost certainly demolished to make way for The First Pike.

This was erected by public subscription to commemorate the surrender of Paris to the Allies in March 1814. The completed Pike was 37 yards 2 feet 4 inches high. Although constructed on a square base about 4 yards high, it was predominantly a circular structure, with a tapering cone at the top. The monument contained about 156 steps which ran precariously around the inside, quite innocent of any bannister rail! This was not an ascent for the giddy or faint hearted! After enduring this ordeal the visitor to the Pike might rest in a small room at the top which contained a fireplace, before plucking up courage for the even more unnerving descent.

The career of the first pike was ill-fated and short lived. Then, as now, vandalism took its toll. Steps were removed and the place was generally wrecked. The authorities walled up the entrance. The final act in the saga took place on the afternoon of Wednesday 8th February 1854, when the inhabitants of the whole area were unnerved by a rumbling sound resembling an earthquake. A glance at the skyline provided the answer: the Pike had fallen down. The collapse was attributed to the structure having been weakened by lightning, which had cracked the walls some years previously. The locals however, were believing none of this. By an unhappy co-incidence the Pike had fallen at the very moment when the Russian Ambassador left London before the declaration of war with Russia. The reason for the fall of the Pike was obvious: it was an omen. Thus did Stoodley Pike find itself saddled with the myth that its collapse heralds the onset of war!

The Pike did not stay ruined for long. On 10th March 1854, a meeting was held in the Golden Lion in Todmorden with the object of rebuilding it. Various meetings followed, and to cut a long story short, money was raised, an architect (Mr James Green) appointed, and work begun. The new Monument was erected further back from the edge of the hill than its predecessor, to avoid the storm erosion on the face of the moor which had weakened the base of the first Pike. The building contractor was Mr Lewis Crabtree of Hebden Bridge.

The present Pike can speak for itself. The massive, badly eroded inscription over the door was carved by Mr Luke Fielden and, surrounded with masonic symbolism, it tells its story as follows:

STOODLEY PIKE
A PEACE MONUMENT

Erected by Public Subscription.
Commenced in 1814 to commemorate the surrender
of Paris to the Allies and finished after the battle of Waterloo
when peace was established in 1815.
By a strange coincidence the Pike fell on the day the Russian
Ambassador left London before the declaration of war with Russia in
1854, and it was rebuilt when peace was proclaimed in 1856.
Repaired and lightning conductor fixed. 1889.

Having said our farewells to the Pike, we follow the Pennine Way (and The Fielden Trail) along the ridge to the old packhorse causey at Withens Gate. Here we turn left (onto the Calderdale Way) and proceed a short distance to the "Te Deum" Stone which hides coyly behind a wall. The face of this ancient stone, faintly reminiscent of a Roman altar, is carved with the legend "Te Deum Laudamus" ("We praise thee O Lord"). Here people would give thanks for a safe journey over the moors, and coffins would be rested on the stone as they were carried over the "corpse road" for interment in Heptonstall churchyard. At one time, Heptonstall was the only church in the area, so it was by no means unusual for corpses to be carried over the moors.

Following the Calderdale Way down towards Green Withens Reservoir our route passes through a landscape of derelict farms, shattered intake walls and upland pastures fast returning to moorland and bog. Here, even in summer, it is decidedly wet underfoot. Following the Calderdale Way Waymarks, turn left, following an old causey which contours the hillside alongside a wall. After a succession of stiles, at a junction of grassy tracks by a trough, turn right, following a grassy track down the hillside to the Reservoir Road (ravine on the left). On reaching the road bear left alongside the Reservoir to the dam and Reservoir Keeper's cottages. From here a metalled road leads without complication to the Hinchcliffe Arms in Cragg Vale.

At Cragg Vale we are back in "Coiner's Country". In the Hinchcliffe Arms there is a small display of some of the tools of the coiner's trade. The Hinchcliffes were the local millowners hereabouts, and Cragg Vale was once notorious for the child labour in its mills, the 1833 commission describing Cragg Vale as "the blackest place of all". The adjacent church of St John-in-the-Wilderness was built in 1815 and Jimmy Savile OBE is one of its churchwardens. The early records of this church reveal appalling mortality rates among the children of Cragg Vale. The grasping millmasters hereabouts were, it seems, just as greedy as their coining predecessors!

Just beyond the Hinchcliffe Arms turn left opposite the Church following the "Calderdale Way Link Path" through meadows by the brook to a stone bridge. Beyond the bridge a track ascends through houses to Cragg Road. Cross the Cragg Road and follow a track which passes between Twist Clough and Mid Birks Cottages. Beyond Upper Birks cottages, turn left, following a path which leads into the woodlands below Robin Hood Rocks.

In the woods here is Spa Laithe, once the venue for an annual well dressing ceremony, and in the eighteenth century the scene of a dramatic arrest. As mentioned, Dighton's murderers, Thomas and Normanton had been acquitted due to the unreliable testimony of the informer Broadbent. Further information however, was to lead to their re-arrest, this time on charges of highway robbery. On 4th May 1774 Thomas confessed to the murder, but Normanton remained silent. On 6th August 1774 Thomas was hanged on Knavesmire and his body tarred and suspended in chains on Beacon Hill, Halifax. Normanton, (incredibly) was allowed out on bail until the next Assizes. Not surprisingly, considering that his friend was by now being eaten by the crows on Beacon Hill, Normanton did not put in an appearance in March 1775, but he sent a plea of guilty. He was sentenced to death in his absence, and the men sent to arrest him found him here at Spa Laithe. There was a chase, and Normanton escaped into the wood, but he was finally caught hiding behind some briars at the bottom of a wall. On 15th April 1775 Normanton confessed on his way to the gallows. On 17th April he joined his accomplice on Beacon Hill. The final act of the coiners tragedy had been played out.

Ignore the path leading onwards into the woods and take the path on the right which ascends steeply to the outcrop of rocks. On reaching the top turn left alongside the wall to a second group of rocks (note the unfinished millstone still attached to the bedrock). Continue onwards through the top of the woods crossing a small stream. Beyond the next stile (holly bush) a track descends the hillside to the left between trees and scrub. On reaching a bothy continue onwards along a grassy terrace to enter Hall Bank Lane at a stile and gate.

Turn left down Hall Bank Lane, which, after meeting the track from Hollin Hey on the left, becomes metalled and descends the hillside without complication back to Mytholmroyd.

Reaching the edge of Mytholmroyd we pass New House on the right (its fine porch is dated 1718). Here lived Thomas Spencer, the brother-in-law of "King David". An ex soldier, he escaped the fate of his compatriots, only to be hanged on Beacon Hill in 1783 for leading a corn riot in Halifax. Spencer's body was afterwards brought home and left on view at Hall Gate. A nineteenth century witness, who saw this as a child, reported that Spencer's neck was level with his chin.

And so, opposite the fine mullions of Mytholmroyd Farm, we reach the end of our journey. A left turn onto the Cragg Road leads back to your car.

New House Mytholmroyd

J.F.J.
1989

7: WAINHOUSE TOWER, HALIFAX

Crags, canal, nature trails, a seventeenth century mansion, and a model village are all to be found on this semi-urban ramble around the edges of the Calder Valley. At the heart of the walk stands the lofty Wainhouse Tower, one of the best known follies in Britain.

Getting there:	From Halifax follow the A629 Huddersfield Road. After descending Salterhebble Hill, turn right for Greetland. Pass over the canal and river and continue onwards, passing under a railway before the road winds right into West Vale. At traffic lights, turn right, then right again into the West Vale car park, which is sited by the entrance to Clay House Park and the North Dean nature trails. Parking is free and there are public conveniences and shops adjacent.
Distance:	6 miles approx.
Map ref:	SE 097 214 Outdoor Leisure 21 or Landranger 104
Rating:	Walk ** Folly and general interest ***

Wainhouse Tower is open to the public at certain times of the year as follows:

> May Day - 1st May
> Spring Bank - Sunday & Monday
> Father's Day (June)
> Show Day (August)
> August Bank - Sunday & Monday
> September Break- Sunday

Admission 40p. Brochures & postcards available. (For full details of the opening times at any given time contact Calderdale Leisure Services on Halifax 59494.)

The Upper Calder Valley boasts two fine follies - Stoodley Pike Monument and the Wainhouse Tower. Of these, Wainhouse Tower

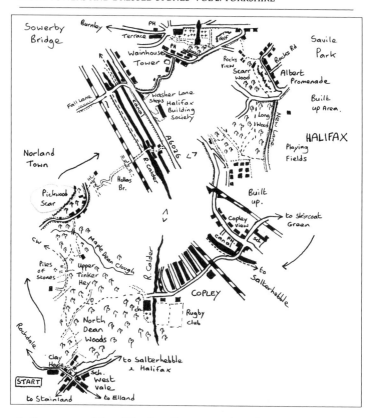

is the most striking. The Stoodley Pike Monument stands remote and aloof, lost in its moorlands and only really making its presence felt in the landscape around Todmorden. The Wainhouse Tower on the other hand was built at the edge of Skircoat Green, at the limit of Halifax's urban sprawl. It stands on the lip of the Calder Valley, a domineering master to the residents of Sowerby Bridge who, immured in the valley far below seem to scurry about their daily affairs like so many tiny ants! It is difficult not to notice the Wainhouse Tower, yet few people who pass by seem to stop to make a closer inspection. Despite "open days", a "History Trail",

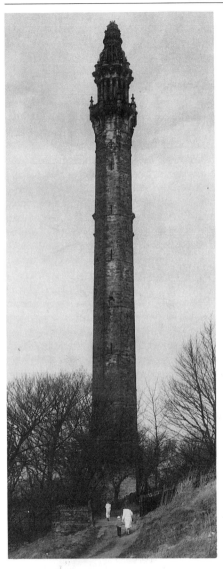

Wainhouse Tower, Halifax

explanatory leaflets in Tourist Information Centres, and improved accessibility, the myths surrounding the Wainhouse Tower still persist and proliferate!

Let me explain what I mean. About two years ago I was travelling home to Mytholmroyd on the train, having spent most of the day in Bradford. In front of me were sitting two rough looking men. They were not together. The dark haired man in the donkey jacket was sitting by the window, whereas the other man, gypsy like, with waistcoat, neck scarf and battered trilby was of that type who sits down next to you on buses and trains and insists (loudly!) on making conversation. As we crossed the viaduct by Copley the Wainhouse Tower came into view. Mr. Donkey Jacket, whose

63

conversation thus far had not really progressed beyond "yus" and "erm" suddenly became more animated:

"Well what's that then up theer? I've allus wondered abaht yon tower; I once heard tell that it were...."

"That's t'Tower o' Spite pal. You've not heard o't'Tower o' Spite?? It were this feller, Lord Halifax, built it to spoil his neighbour's view. It seems him an' his neighbour fell aht ovver a woman, an t' lass killed herself by jumpin' off o' t'tower. Tower o' spite that pal.... Tower o' spite."

I cannot recall the conversation that followed. Suffice it to say that it was the most fanciful fabrication I had ever heard, and by the time I got off the train at Mytholmroyd, I was heartily regretting that I could not continue on to Todmorden, as I would have loved to have listened in on the cock and bull story he no doubt must have concocted to explain away the presence of Stoodley Pike. However, this little incident graphically demonstrates the myths that cling to the Wainhouse Tower in particular and to follies in general.

It is curious that this gentleman mentioned someone jumping off the tower. A Canadian Newspaper, *The Sun*, recently ran a picture of the Wainhouse Tower with the headline "TOWER OF DEATH". According to this account the tower was built in Budapest in 1504 as a memorial to a victorious general! The story goes that a merchant, eager to marry the "other woman" lured his wife to the top, and pushed her over the balustrade. The merchant was brought to trial and sentenced to the same death as his victim. From then on the tower became the regular venue for executions, and thousands of malefactors ascended the tower's 400 steps to be thrown to their deaths on the rocks below! The story only appeared locally when the picture of the tower was noticed by a Mrs Sylvia Ward, who had emigrated to Canada from Halifax in 1974. She brought the article back home, and the local press had a good laugh at it. Still, it makes you wonder about what you read in the papers!

Our journey to the Wainhouse Tower begins at West Vale car park. Cross the footbridge over the beck into Clay House Park, skirt the edge of the playing field and ascend the steps through the gardens to Clay House.

Clay House is a striking seventeenth-century residence with an old barn, and it is no surprise to learn that it was once the homestead of the Clay Family. In 1957 there was some speculation that this

Penhill Preceptory

Follies of Sorrelsykes Park near Aysgarth.
Top left: A sham ruin Top right: The Rocket Bottom left: The Pepper Pot
Bottom right: The Summer House at Swinithwaite Hall

might have been the site of the long lost Roman Cambodunum when a Roman altar (dating from AD 208) was found hereabouts. It was dedicated to the local goddess Victoria Brigantia, and is now in the Fitzwilliam Museum in Cambridge. A replica remains.

Clay House has a visitor centre and is also the starting point of the 50-mile-long Calderdale Way which was opened in October 1978 - a challenging expedition if you can spare the time!

Pass between Clay House and Clay House Barn to a track. Bear right then left, following a well defined nature trail into North Dean Woods, following the course of the former Lancashire and Yorkshire railway line to Holywell Green. North Dean Woods is predominantly oak and birch, especially the latter, which once clothed the whole valley long ago. In the eighteenth century the North Dean Wood Charity eased the lot of the local poor with profits derived from the sale of the wood's timber.

At the first junction of paths, take the left fork, ascending the woods, passing waymarks and a curiously carved boulder en route. On reaching a stile at the top of the woods bear right, following the line of the Calderdale Way along the top of the wood. At the next junction of paths (by a cottage) take the left fork again, continuing along the top of the woods until the path climbs steeply up old quarry delfs beyond a stile (numerous piles of boulders adjacent, probably cleared from neighbouring pastures).

Quarrying is a venerable industry hereabouts, although happily it no longer scars the landscape in the way it once did. Many quarries have disappeared under landfill, and the few that still operate (around the Shibden Valley for example) are carefully regulated. Here, above the Calder, the stone has been quarried from the outcrops on the valley edges and has left indelible scars. The local millstone grit (known as the Elland Flags) is very resistant to sea erosion, and consequently has been exported for use in harbours all over the world. In Calcutta, Hong Kong, Sydney and Copenhagen you will find Halifax stone, as you will in the War Office and the British Museum. If ever we find a city on Mars you can bet your boots that its streets will be paved with Elland flags!

It is also thanks to the local revolution in quarrying (which began in the early seventeenth century) that there are so many fine stone houses in the area dating from this period. These "Halifax houses" with their fine mullioned and transomed windows, with gables topped by ball finials, must surely represent an architectural style that is unique to this area. If you look at Thomas Jeffery's map of the district, which was drawn in 1775, you see the Calderdale hillsides thickly packed with these farmsteads, whereas Bradford is little more than a village, and smaller than Halifax! The reason is that prior to the Industrial Revolution Halifax lay at the centre of an enormous domestic based textile industry, so typified by those tenter frames decked out with cloth "pieces" which Defoe so vividly described on his journey over the "mountains" to "Hallifax" in the eighteenth century. All these farms were busily engaged in spinning and weaving, and in taking their finished cloth to Halifax Market.

It is ironic that when Halifax opened its new custom built "Piece Hall" in 1779 this old established way of life was already standing on the brink of its own extinction! Machines, mills, canals and railways were to create new towns where formerly there were villages, and the upland farmsteads would be left to fall into decay as the population progressively moved downhill to where the work was. This pattern has remained right down to the 1980s, and only now, with the arrival of affluent "yuppy" outsiders are the hills starting to be repopulated. Tourists throng around Walkley's Clog Factory at Hebden Bridge. "Peg rugs" sell in trendy craft shops for astronomical sums (in the 1950s my mum used to make them because we couldn't afford a "proper" rug). The rough stoneware pottery, which our parents threw out in favour of Staffordshire china, is today the tableware of the affluent and mill bobbins make upmarket tourist souvenirs. It is ironic that the symbols of former poverty should today be equated with middle class trendiness. To my parents and grandparents all these things were (and still are) junk: mute symbols of the poverty and the hardships they had to endure in the mills, quarries, mines and back-to-back slums of the black industrial West Riding.

As we walk along the hillsides around Norland the slumbering memories of this upland landscape are neatly dovetailed with all the evidences of urban development in the valley below. Those evidences are everywhere. Copley, like a small version of Bradford's Saltaire, was a custom built community centred on its mill. The canal runs alongside the river, and the magnificent (or repulsive - depending how you look at it!) 23 arch Copley Railway Viaduct tells of the coming of the Lancashire and Yorkshire Railway in 1852.

The pattern continues down to the present day. The latest "beautification" to grace this section of the Calder valley is the New Halifax Building Society Computer Centre which was completed in 1989. This drab building has but one saving grace - the fine drystone walling around it was built by Ray Howarth, a shepherd brought up on a hill farm tucked beneath Erringden Moor, who when not grazing his sheep on Oldtown Cricket Pitch near Hebden Bridge, builds walls and breeds budgies. The walls belong to the Pennine landscape, their stones spring from it in an elemental way. The nineteenth century builders of mills and chapels knew this, which was why they built in ashlar and millstone grit. It seems to me that today's architects, armed with methods and materials that have not yet withstood the test of time are fated to learn the lessons of our forefathers the hard way!

Beyond the quarries, descending to the pasture again, a gate stile appears in the fence on the right. (The Calderdale Way carries straight on.) Turn right, descending the steep path to the bottom of the wood. A footpath which leads off left has been blocked. Instead turn right, down towards Upper Tinker Hey. Just before reaching the house turn left down to the wall end, then left again along a paved "causey" which leads to a fine footbridge over Maple Dean Clough. Ascend to the cottages on Dye House Lane below Pickwood Scar. Bear right along Moor End Lane, passing Puntle Hall and Pickwood Nurseries. Where the lane winds round to left, beyond houses, a stile leads to an overgrown footpath on the right. Follow the footpath to join a lane by a farm. Turn right then left, following the overgrown (and muddy!) Hollas Lane down the hillside, passing through two stiles, before entering a track by the railway line, where a notice informs us that the path was restored in autumn 1988 by W.H.Smith School, Brighouse.

Pass under the railway and continue onwards to Sterne bridge over the Calder by a weir (Standard Wire Co. opposite). Do not cross the river; instead turn left along a well defined footpath along the riverbank. This leads without complication to the next bridge by the junction of Mereclough Road and Fall Lane, by the household waste site on the outskirts of Sowerby Bridge.

Sowerby Bridge is a product of the Industrial Revolution. It was originally just a river crossing, the hub of civilisation being the village of Sowerby, on the adjacent hillside. The Industrial Revolution changed all that and Sowerby Bridge grew into a mill town, leaving

Sowerby as an outlying satellite.

Despite the later impact of the railway, Sowerby Bridge's real history began with the arrival of the canal. Its canal basin marks the limit of the Calder and Hebble Navigation and the start of the transpennine Rochdale Canal. The Calder and Hebble was surveyed by John Smeaton in 1757 and opened to Sowerby Bridge Wharf in 1770. Smeaton was of course the builder of the first Eddystone Lighthouse, and in 1756, when first approached by the local canal promoters, he had been at Plymouth engaged upon that project. The Rochdale Canal reached the Sowerby Bridge basin in 1798.

With the arrival of the railways Sowerby Bridge gradually turned its back on the canal, and, although in commercial use right down to the 1940s the waterways were gradually allowed to fall into decay, the Rochdale in particular becoming a repository for all the rubbish of the neighbourhood. Happily, the Calder and Hebble was spared the worst excesses of the decline. Where the commercial traffic left off the tourist traffic took over, and the Sowerby Bridge Basin was gradually developed into the fine marina it is today. The Rochdale was less fortunate - its locks were capped with concrete and sections of it were filled in and culverted. The rubbish and the weed did the rest. Throughout the 1980s however, the Rochdale has been undergoing restoration and is once more navigable for most of its length. In Sowerby Bridge though, the canal is still culverted beneath Tuel Lane and a car park, but there are grandiose plans for "a Tunnel under Tuel" and it seems likely that the Rochdale will soon be joined up to the national network again. Today Sowerby Bridge is very much a community in decline. This is sad for a town which once boasted that if it could be bought, somebody in Sowerby Bridge was manufacturing it! We can only hope that better times lie ahead.

At Mereclough Road turn right over the river and the canal. (If you wish to include Sowerby Bridge in the walk, turn left along the canal towpath to reach Sowerby Bridge Basin a short distance along the canal. After exploring Sowerby Bridge retrace your steps.) Turn right again up Canal Lane, and cross the busy Wakefield Road to Washer Lane, where a road sign warns us to beware of Toads!

Ascend Washer Lane, winding left, then right, to its junction with Darcy Hey Lane and Upper Washer Lane, opposite the Folly Hotel. Turn right up Upper Washer Lane to the Wainhouse Tower.

After the rural delights of the Norland side of the valley, the landscape hereabouts is suburban to say the least, and if a visit to the Wainhouse Terrace is contemplated the busy A58 road will need to be negotiated.

The Wainhouse Tower is 253 feet high and contains over 400 steps. It is estimated to contain over 9000 tons of material. The view from the top is phenomenal, as is the change of climate. I once went up the tower in a tee shirt on a warm summer's day when people were sunbathing on the grass below, only to find myself chilled by an icy biting wind which was howling around the observation platform. Ascending the tower is an interesting (and tiring) experience.

Now for the true story of the Wainhouse Tower, which is also known as the Octagon Tower, Wainhouse Folly, the Observatory and J.E.W.'s Folly. John Edward Wainhouse was born in 1817 and worked in his uncle's dyeworks at Washer Lane. On the death of his

uncle in 1856, Wainhouse inherited the dyeworks together with various other properties. It is not known whether or not he personally ran the dyeworks but in 1870 he leased the premises to one Henry Mossman. Now Wainhouse's wealthy neighbour was Sir Henry Edwards, who resided at nearby Pye Nest, and it is said that Wainhouse constructed the tower out of spite against this man, with whom he had an ongoing feud. This is not strictly true, but the legend is not entirely without foundation as we shall see.

The fact is that the Wainhouse Tower is actually a chimney. There was no real mystery attached to it, it was simply built to serve the Washer Lane dyeworks as part of an early attempt to combat atmospheric pollution! In those days Halifax was a black industrial town frequently blanketed with smog for days on end (even in the 1950s Halifax was a black, grimy town!). It might seem surprising therefore, to think that there was concern about atmospheric pollution in the dark days of the nineteenth century, but concern there indeed was, and Smoke Abatement Acts had already been passed by Parliament. This is where Edwards' first comes into the picture. He complained to the authorities about the smoke from the Washer Lane Dyeworks, and it was in response to this that Wainhouse set about building his chimney. If there was a feud between Wainhouse and Edwards, this was no doubt the point at which it began.

John Edward Wainhouse set out to build a chimney which would stand well above the smoke nuisance level, some 350 yards or so up the hillside from the dyeworks, connected to it by an underground flue. He employed a local architect, Isaac Booth (who was also Edwards' architect!), to build for him a chimney which would do the job without appearing ugly. Booth designed a conventional circular chimney with an octagonal stone casing and a spiral staircase running between the two. He planned to cap the whole thing with a pedimented balcony. Why there needed to be a staircase is a total mystery. It could have served no useful purpose, especially if smoke was belching out of the chimney. Even at the planning stage the structure was in danger of becoming a folly. Building of the tower began in 1871. Stone was hauled up the inside of the chimney by a tripod set up on top of the structure. One of the blocks of stone which held the winch can still be seen near the tower entrance. At one point the tripod collapsed and a large stone fell on to the foreman's son, Isaac Buckley, who lost an arm as a result.

In 1873 there was a change of tack. Sir Henry Edwards, who was known to be a boastful man, bragged that from no house on the hills around his Pye Nest estates could anybody get a view of his private gardens. It seems that Wainhouse planned to alter this state of affairs by building an observatory on the top of his chimney! Wainhouse had to employ a new architect. Booth was getting fed up with the feud and could no longer brook being the servant of two warring masters. He was caught in the crossfire and had had enough. In his stead Wainhouse appointed his assistant, Richard Swarbrick Dugdale, who completely redesigned the upper section of the tower. He created a two-tier structure with large lower and smaller upper balustraded balconies. The whole thing was surmounted with a lantern dome and finial.

The building was finally completed in September 1875. It was fated never to be used as a chimney. Even before its completion this had become obvious, as Wainhouse had finally sold the dyeworks to Mossman, and the tower was not included in the deal! The struggle over the smoke from Washer Lane Dyeworks continued unabated, but Wainhouse's Tower no longer had any role in the proceedings. It had already transcended the status of mere chimney.

John Edward Wainhouse died in 1883. Since then his tower has had mixed fortunes. In 1893 it revealed its true nature when it was leased to Joe Brook Carrier at a rent of £15 per annum. He employed it for its only useful purpose, simply opening it to the public and charging a small fee to ascend the tower! By 1893 there was talk of demolishing it but mercifully this did not happen. At the turn of the century the entrance to the tower was used as a hen hut, and in 1909 a Mr P.Denison was using it as an aerial for radio transmissions. In 1912 it was suggested that the tower be used as a crematorium, an idea no doubt inspired by the adjacent graveyard, but thankfully this came to nothing. In World War Two the tower was used as an ARP observation post, and in 1963 it acquired a white CND sign, which has since been painted out. On royal occasions the top of the tower is sometimes illuminated, the last time this happened being in 1977 for the Queen's Silver Jubilee.

I need hardly mention that the view from the top of the tower is excellent, and Stoodley Pike, the Jubilee Tower, the Whitley Moor Gazebo and the Emley Moor Transmitter are all visible from the viewing balcony.

The tower is not Wainhouse's only monument. His house, "West Air", is now the "Royal Hotel", (recently renamed "The Folly") and the Wainhouse Terrace Colonnade stands beside the A646 Burnley Road, being, despite the hazards of the A58, well worth the necessary detour. The colonnade was stone cleaned in 1973. Across the road stands another curiosity - a mullioned and transomed seventeenth-century frontage now incorporated into a retaining wall. This stands beneath the modern New Allan Fold Inn. We must assume that this is all that remains of the "Old Allan Fold".

Retracing our steps to the Wainhouse Tower we proceed up Wakefield Gate, passing a quarry with sheds on the left. From here back to North Dean the route is predominantly built up, but not without odd bits of crag, woodland and open space. Nearby is Savile Park, which is Halifax's answer to Harrogate's "Stray", and which is the setting for the odd circus and Halifax's annual show. In days gone by, when it was Skircoat Green, it was a venue for Chartist meetings. It is said that the Chartists smuggled pamphlets into Halifax in a coffin and met at the Standard of Freedom Inn not far distant. The Green was given to the town in 1866 by Captain Savile who sold his manorial rights for the sum of £100 on condition that the council would do something about smoke abatement in the area!

Pass through a small stile on the right, descending a slope to a track behind terrace housing. Pass the terrace of Rocks View on the right, and follow a path along hillside to a stile which enters a cobbled track adjacent to the Albert Promenade. Here there are crags and trees, and a potential playground for the rock climber. Walk along Albert Promenade, or follow the woodland path below the crags to Birdcage Hill. Beyond, a path leads through Long Wood, finally descending to the A6026 by Copley Viaduct.

Turn left along the road, passing under the viaduct. Proceed into the village and turn right down Copley Lane, just past the Volunteer Arms. The Lane crosses the canal and bears right then left under the railway to Copley.

Copley was built between 1847 and 1853 by Colonel Edward Akroyd, who was a worsted manufacturer and founder of the Yorkshire Penny Bank. It was a model village, preceding Akroyd's other "model community" of Akroyden, which he sited near his house at Bankfield (now the Halifax Museum). It also predates Sir Titus Salt's model community at Saltaire, and this alone makes it historically important. At Copley Akroyd had a canteen shed where 600 workmen could be served dinners of meat and potatoes at 2d a throw. The mill was built in 1847 with an 1865 addition, but has since been demolished. Copley had its own school (1849), library (1850), and of course the church, a fine neo-Gothic structure, dedicated to St.Stephen, which stands across the river and was built 1863-5. The architect was W.H.Crossland.

Cross the river, passing the church on the left, then go through a stile (left) into woodland. Ascend diagonally up the wood to a plank bridge by a pond. Turn left onto a well defined path with a retaining wall, following a nature trail through the woods. After ascending the wood to the right to skirt an area of erosion control, another well signed path runs along North Dean Woods, encountering other footpaths en route. The path eventually winds to the right through a cutting, to join with the Calderdale Way behind Clay House. Turn left down a wallside ginnel, passing through an unsightly yard to a gate by the Calderdale Countryside Service Depot. Turn left to the start of the walk at Clay House.

Personally speaking, I do not find this part of Calderdale as attractive as the landscapes further up the valley beyond Luddendenfoot. To me the area is marred by the sewage works, trunk roads and general industrialisation. Nevertheless, it is still well worth a visit, and despite first impressions you will find an interesting, stimulating and generally enjoyable ramble. You will also encounter what must be the finest folly in Northern England. Even if there were nothing else of interest, this alone would make the walk worth undertaking, but there is interest, and lots of it; all you have to do is seek it out!

8: HOYLAND LOWE STAND

A restored and working watermill, a church with interesting monuments, an obelisk in incongruous surroundings, collieries in decline and a mysterious prospect tower are all to be found on this part industrial/part rural ramble through the landscape of the Barnsley Coalfield.

Getting there:	Leave the M1 at Junction 36 and follow A 61 through Birdwell towards Barnsley. Park at Worsborough Mill (3 miles south of Barnsley, 2 miles north of the M1 junction 36) where there is a spacious (free) car park.
Distance:	5$^{1}/_{2}$ miles. Easy enough, but beware of complaining children!
Map Ref:	SE 349 009 Landranger 111
Rating:	Walk ** Follies and General Interest **
	Note: Worsborough Mill open Wednesday to Sunday, 10 am to 5.30 pm.

Worsborough Mill is one of South Yorkshire's industrial archaeological gems. Standing on the banks of the River Dove, it is now incorporated into a 130 acre Country Park. The mill, after being in use for over 300 years, closed down in the 1960s, only to be restored and re-opened as an industrial museum in 1976. It has a venerable pedigree. A corn mill at Worsborough is mentioned in the Domesday Book of 1086, and no doubt there was a mill here right down to around 1625, when the present mill was constructed. The Industrial Revolution and the subsequent expansion of local coal and iron working increased demand for bread to such an extent that a second (steam powered) mill was added to the original complex in 1843. The decline of Worsborough Mill was brought about by the introduction of modern roller milling and the consequent change in public taste from stoneground to cheap, mass produced white flour. By the 1920s the steam engine had been scrapped and the watermill had been reduced to producing animal feed. Happily the recent

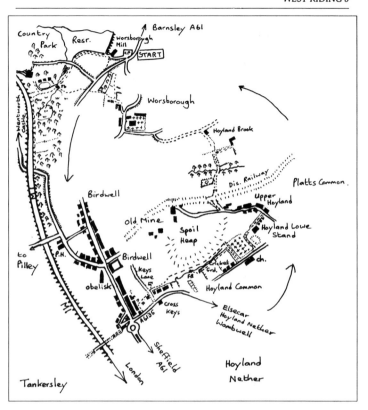

restoration, along with the resurgence of interest in wholefood products, has ensured that the mill is not only a living, working museum but also a thriving concern, selling the flour it produces. Today a Hornsby oil engine, built in 1911, drives the old steam mill, and this, along with the original water-wheel, effectively demonstrates to children where our "daily bread" comes from.

Our walk starts at the rear of Worsborough Mill. Cross the bridge over the mill race and follow a track through the woods, with the reservoir on the right. Beyond, a stile and footbridge appear on the left, along with an area of boggy ground. Ignore this route (which leads up to the main road and

Worsborough) and instead continue onwards, following a made up gravel path which leads through woods, passing a marsh on the left, to the embankment of the M1.

Motorways are nasty, noisy places which have a habit of bringing out the worst in human nature. How amazing it is, therefore, to discover that lurking beneath the high embankments of this throbbing, humming artery of human insanity is a backwater of sylvan beauty, a habitat for birds, wild animals and flowering plants! The effect of building the M1 has been to bottle up water behind its earthwork base, and to produce a series of reed choked marsh-girt ponds, which make a perfect natural habitat for wildfowl. It seems that the M1 does some good after all!

Now we follow a path along the base of the embankment with a reedy lake on the left. This leads through woodlands to join Rockley Lane by the motorway underpass. Turn left and follow the Rockley Abbey/Wentworth Castle road which winds uphill, passing a motorway bridge and the Cock Inn to emerge into the A61 at Grimy Birdwell.

The pits at Birdwell have gone, but what Worsborough has turned into an industrial museum Birdwell has turned into an industrial estate! Red brick Birdwell straggles along the A61, an unlovely reminder that Barnsley's mucky past has not yet been totally consigned to photographs in history books.

Where the Rockley Abbey/Wentworth Castle road joins the A61 at Birdwell we encounter our first folly - a tall obelisk, sited incongruously in a haulier's yard. Towering over the roaring carriageways of the M1 and surrounded by decaying vehicles, this must surely be the most unloved obelisk in Yorkshire. The obelisk is, in fact, little more than a direction pointer. The carved inscription says "Wentworth Castle 3 miles 1775". Wentworth Castle (not to be confused with Wentworth Woodhouse), is back down the road on which we came, and more follies may be found in its grounds (see appendix).

At the obelisk turn right, along the busy A61, and follow to the road junction at the end of the village (passing the Yoga Centre on the right). Turn left onto the A6135, signed Chapeltown, Elsecar, Hoyland Nether. The departure from Birdwell is uninspiring. The construction of industrial units has diverted the footpath, and the route leads behind them, knee deep in rubbish! A few yards beyond the junction turn immediately left, following an untidy footpath behind an industrial site. At the first stile turn right, and proceed across pastures to enter Cross Keys Lane from a particularly elusive stile.

Cross the lane and continue onwards, following a signed footpath uphill, passing industry and allotments on the right. At a footbridge over a stream cross it and bear left up the inside of the fence (right of way), or alternatively simply follow the well defined path running along the side of the adjacent pit heap. Now we are back in a countryside of sorts ascending alongside the pit heap behind Hoyland Common. At the brow of the hill, turn right and follow the track to Hoyland Nether, emerging onto the B6096 opposite St Peter's Church. Turn left, then beyond the cemetery turn left again, following a nettle choked path round the far side of the graveyard to Hoyland Lowe Stand.

Hoyland Lowe Stand

Hoyland Lowe Stand is, like all good follies, a total enigma. It is not at all clear who built it or why. With sightless bricked up windows, it is essentially a two storeyed square tower, with a higher stair turret, not unlike Boot's Folly (see Appendix). By all accounts it was built as a "hunting stand" - a lookout tower connected with the chase. Pevsner gives a date of c.1720 but we get the feeling that he is merely guessing! The Stand is quite visible from the hillside above Elsecar, which suggests a possible association with the Marquis of Rockingham's follies at Wentworth Woodhouse, but then again the Stand is equally prominent when viewed from Worsborough. We are left with a mystery.

From Hoyland Lowe Stand, continue downhill, bravely negotiating a path choked with jungle weeds and garden refuse which soon enters a metalled lane. Turn left and pass through Upper Hoyland. Where the road bears left towards a derelict colliery by a farm, continue onwards, following a rough track down to a disused railway embankment. After crossing the disused railway line the path leads past filter beds to a wood and a stream, then ascends between hedges, finally leading up fields to meet a farm road at Hoyland Brook Cottage. Turn left along the farm track to enter Worsbrough village alongside the Church.

Worsborough Village is a lovely place where the Barnsley blight seems remote, and we look back to the South Yorkshire of an earlier, pre-industrial age. The church (St Mary's) is particularly worthy of exploration, despite the fact that the author found it locked on two separate visits! If you succeed in getting access you will find a fine Norman chancel and substantial fourteenth-century work. There is a fine eighteenth-century squire's pew, but the most striking feature of the church must surely be the sixteenth-century monument to Roger Rockley. Dating from 1534, the monument is an unusual (and rare) example of the Tudor woodcarver's art. It is essentially a timber bunk bed! On the topmost bunk lies a carved effigy of Roger Rockley, resplendent in his armour, his hands clasped in prayer, and on the bottom bunk lies his withered cadaver, a carved skeleton in gruesome repose. Outside in the churchyard these dire warnings continue, in a less spectacular, but no less interesting manner. On the north side of the church a particularly gaunt gravestone bears the following legend:

In memory of JOSEPH BEAUMONT
Late of Worsborough Bridge, Colliery Manager
who met with a sudden death by an explosion
of fire damp, in Pilley Ironstone Pit
September 16th 1847, aged 55 years.
ALSO JOSEPH, his son, who was thrown from
a horse near Morrow House and survived only
24 hours August 29th 1847 aged 18 years.

The grave also contains another son aged 3 and two daughters aged 13 and 9 respectively. Such tragedies unfold frequently on these cold, unyielding tablets of mossy, hoary stone, which stand as grim monuments to our Victorian ancestors' spiritual aspirations to an eternal afterlife. But such thoughts will not detain you long! The countryside is fair and the last leg of our ramble awaits!

From Worsbrough Church turn right, passing Edmund's Arms on the left. Where the road winds to the right, take the first fork on the left, then turn left by Columbine Cottage. Turn right, (following a sign for Worsborough Mill) passing along the backs of the houses before descending a well marked path through two arable fields. At the bottom of the fields turn left, to enter the busy A621 Sheffield/Barnsley Road through a stile. Cross the main road (with care!) to the stile opposite, then descend the pasture to the next stile which enters the track immediately behind Worsborough Mill.

Worsborough Mill

9: WENTWORTH WOODHOUSE -
Hoober Stand.

Two excellent follies, a fine stately home and a rare Newcomen beam engine are the high points of this fine ramble which explores an unexpectedly beautiful landscape tucked away in the Yorkshire coalfield between Barnsley and Rotherham.

Getting there:	The walk starts in Elsecar. Leave the M1 at junction 36 between Birdwell and Tankersley. On approaching Birdwell turn right onto the A6135 (signed Platt's Common, Elsecar and Hoyland Nether). At traffic lights turn left then take the right fork down through Hoyland Nether to Elsecar. Where the road bends left by Market Inn turn right, then left into the car park opposite Elsecar Park .
Distance:	7 miles. Tiring - not recommended for small children.
Map ref:	SK 385 997 Landranger 111
Rating:	Walk *** Follies. ***

The Yorkshire Coalfield: "muck stacks", allotments, pit villages, racing pigeons, strong ale, rough and ready miners and industrial desolation. These are the images which most frequently spring to mind at the mention of Barnsley or Rotherham. The description is only partially true, for hidden away behind the pit heaps is a hinterland of rolling hills, fine parkland and sweeping views over the surrounding countryside.

Elsecar fits these images. Along with its neighbour, Hoyland Nether, which sprawls all over the hillside, it is neither a linear nor a nucleated community but more a semi urban rag-bag of housing and industrial sites. Were it not for the pleasant countryside over the hill towards Worsborough, you might be forgiven for thinking the whole area was an overspill of Barnsley. The village has a pleasant park which seems almost to be apologising for the

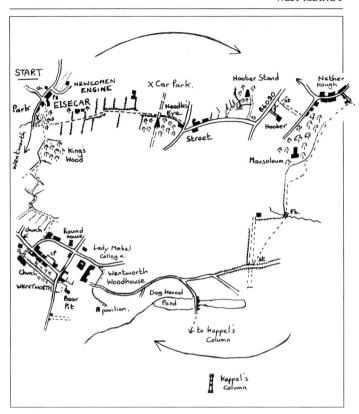

shortcomings of the rest of the community. It's chief jewel is, however, a predictably industrial one. Pass the Market Inn and about 100 yards further on turn right down Distillery Side to reach the Elsecar Engine.

The Elsecar Engine is one of industrial archaeology's showpieces. It is the last Newcomen pumping engine still to be located over its original mineshaft. It was built in 1787 by John Bargh of Chesterfield for Earl Fitzwilliam, but was probably not in actual use until 1795. The original wooden beam of the engine was replaced by a cast iron one with parallel motion in 1836. The cylinder of the engine, which

81

was installed in 1801, is 4 feet in diameter with a 5 foot stroke. It could raise 50 gallons per stroke at a rate of 6 strokes per minute from a depth of 130 feet. The engine worked continuously until 1923 when electric pumps took over. In June 1928, however, the pumps were flooded and the old engine was (temporarily) put back to work. It last ran in 1954.

Industrial Elsecar was very much the handiwork of the Fitzwilliams of Wentworth Woodhouse, who enlarged the village on a planned basis in the middle of the nineteenth century. Their improvements included terraced housing, a steam cornmill, school, church, mineral offices and private railway station. Most of Elsecar was employed in its extensive ironworks. Little trace remains now.

From the car park turn left along the road to cross the stream, then left again following a path between hedgerows. At a junction of paths, ignore the obvious routes to right and left and head straight up the hill. This soon becomes an attractive path ascending through arable fields, with King's Wood to the right, as a fine view opens up behind towards Hoyland, capped by the distant folly of Hoyland Lowe Stand.

The sudden change from a predominantly mining and urban landscape to a rural one is quite unexpected. It is almost as if someone had drawn a line south of Elsecar and said "they shall not pass"!

This is not far from the truth. Wentworth Woodhouse was the abode of the Marquis of Rockingham in the eighteenth century and later the Fitzwilliams, who strenuously resisted any industrial intrusion into their parklands from coal mines or iron workings. Consequently the whole area remains unspoilt. Today, parklands which were once preserved for the exclusive pleasure of the rich are now a playground for the citizens of Rotherham and Barnsley, who make no effort to advertise to outsiders the existence of these hidden attractions.

The Rockinghams were not, however, merely content with deer parks. They had a taste for the bizarre. A pretty horizon was not enough; the eighteenth century was the Age of Reason, which saw the universe as a well regulated mechanism infallible in its perfection. Simplicity and good taste were the order of the day, and above all neatness and control. Wentworth Woodhouse is a statement in stone of power and wealth, but above all it is about control. The eighteenth-century mind sought order. It marvelled at the awesome power of nature, but preferred to keep that power at arm's length. To the eighteenth-century aristocrat nature in the raw was a peepshow, a "look but don't touch" phenomenon. You might visit the "terrible precipices" of Goredale Scar, and then return home to re-create them (on a smaller and safer scale of course) in your own back garden, but that was as far as your interest in nature went!

You could build grottoes, lakes and fountains, architectural toys to amuse your guests, but the overall message was always the same - order out of chaos, man's complete control over the natural environment. Nature was aped, mocked and reduced to a scale calculated to delight but never to overawe. Conversely, architectural achievements were designed to do just the opposite, and to dominate the surrounding landscape with their presence. The eighteenth-century nobleman had to find a way of making his mark on the world, to build shrines to those deities of reason, order and control upon which his position rested. A feudal baron would have built a castle, the Rockinghams built follies.

The first folly takes us by surprise. Passing under power lines, Keppel's Column appears in the far distance, and ahead, Hoober Stand may be seen amongst trees. But as the path meets woodland on the right, the Needle's Eye is unexpectedly encountered through a gap in the woodland perimeter.

The Needle's Eye is a high arch surmounted by a pyramid straddling a long grassy corridor which descends the hillside to Wentworth Woodhouse. It was built around 1780 by the 2nd Marquis of Rockingham, reputedly in order to win a wager! Rockingham, besides being a folly builder extraordinaire, also had a reputation for being a bit of a gambler. (It is said that he once staked £500 on a race between five turkeys and five geese from Norwich to London!) The Needle's Eye was the outcome of one such bet - one night the Marquis boasted that he was such a fine coachman he could drive a coach and four through the "eye of a needle". His friends of course immediately offered a wager which the Marquis accepted, no doubt soberly awakening to the full realisation of his folly the following day. But Rockingham was not a man to be easily defeated. Summoning his architect (John Carr) he ordered construction of a "Needle's Eye", with an archway just wide enough to pass a coach and four! Needless to say he won his

The Needle's Eye

bet and the "Needle's Eye" still stands, a mute reminder of an old man's folly!

Retracing your steps to the path, follow it along the estate perimeter until tarmac is reached on Coaley Lane. Turn right, then quickly left along Street Lane to Street (on a Roman road perhaps?). Just beyond the last row of cottages a sign marks a footpath on the left, which leads up fields to where a stile gives access to a wood. In the wood bear half left, breasting a small hillock to arrive at the unmistakable and lugubrious folly of Hoober Stand.

Hoober Stand must surely rate as one of the finest follies in Britain. Gaunt and black, it eludes architectural definition. It is a

massive structure of gross ugliness. From a distance it looks like a
sad and forlorn windmill, stripped of its sails and shrouded by
trees, but a closer examination reveals it to be no such thing. Over
100 feet in height and built of a yellowstone which the smoke of
South Yorkshire has long since blackened, Hoober Stand is quite
unashamedly a belvedere, a prospect tower topped by iron railings
and a round pavilion like structure, which was presumably the
point of emergence for the now inaccessible internal staircase of 155
spiral steps. The most amazing thing about Hoober Stand (apart
from its sheer size) is the fact that contrary to all appearances the
building has only three sides. Its shape and situation suggest four,
and the taking in of the building's true dimensions is something of
a conceptual feat!

Hoober Stand belongs to the earlier generation of Wentworth
Woodhouse follies. Designed by Henry Flitcroft (who was also
responsible for Fort Belvedere in Windsor Great Park) it was built
in 1748 by the first Marquess of Rockingham, to celebrate the defeat
of Bonnie Prince Charlie at Culloden and to commemorate the
peace treaty of Aix-La-Chapelle. The building is now in a dangerous
condition, with trees growing out of the stone pediment over the
doorway, where a disintegrating inscription records that:

1748

This pyramidall building was erected

by his Majestie's moft dutyfull subject

THOMAS, Marquefs of ROCKINGHAM

in Grateful Respect to the Preserver of our Religion, Laws and Libertys

KING GEORGE THE SECOND

who by ye majesty of God having subdued ye most unnatural Rebellion

in Britain Anno 1746

Maintains the balance of power and settles

a Just and Honourable Peace in Europe.

1748.

Hoober Stand is an amazing and unique building, which should
not be allowed to fall into such decay. Neither is it falling down
alone, for neglect and oblivion seems to be the fate of all the
Wentworth Woodhouse follies. One can only hope that these
remarkable structures will be restored to their former glory before
it is too late.

Hoober
Stand.

J. Jones 1989

From Hoober Stand our route leads onwards to Nether Haugh, with Keppel's Column visible on the hillside opposite. This is perhaps the best known of the Wentworth Woodhouse follies, but to include it turns a pleasant ramble into a blistering hike - so we'll reserve it for another day. *Beyond Hoober Stand bear right, following a shady path straight down the hillside to rejoin the lane. Turn left, and follow the lane to the B6090. At the road turn left again, passing a cottage with a fine sundial (note "Rotherham Roundwalk" waymarks). Soon, a Footpath sign on the right gives access to a small woodland. Pass through a stile and cross a field to another stile consisting of two neatly dressed stone stoops. Here ignore the path leading on towards Stubbin and turn right, down the field edge, passing Hoober to emerge onto the B6091 in a flurry of pigmuck! Turn left, and follow the road to Nether Haugh (note the stunning topiary at "Thistledoo").*

On reaching the B6089 (Rotherham-Wombwell) road, turn right into Nether Haugh. On the bend (near a partially ruined building which looks like it might have had a bell tower), turn right, down a track, and just beyond the last building, by fields, turn right once more, following a path along the edge of woodland. Below, on the left, lakes may be seen. Soon the Wentworth Woodhouse Mausoleum appears in adjacent woodland (private). The Mausoleum was built in 1788 by John Carr, it is a domed three storeyed structure with Corinthian columns. Inside, I am informed, is a statue of the second Marquess of Rockingham by Nollekens dated 1774. This is surrounded by busts of the Marquess' friends: Keppel, Fox, the Duke of Portland, Burke etc.

Bear left down the hillside, to a plank bridge over a small stream. From here a path leads to the Wentworth Woodhouse Drive, near Dog Kennel Pond. Turn right, and follow the drive to Wentworth Woodhouse Park. Entering the deer park, our walk passes an Ionic rotunda on the left, before at last approaching Wentworth Woodhouse itself. Here is a most striking mansion. Its east front is around 600 feet long, which must make it the longest front of any British stately home. It is also a most unusual edifice in that it is not one but two eighteenth-century mansions merging into each other. Wentworth Woodhouse is built on two levels, and incorporated into the earlier of the two mansions are the remains of the original seventeenth-century house of Thomas Wentworth, the Earl of Strafford who was beheaded in 1641. As there is no direct way around them, the two mansions can never be seen together, and there is in fact a difference of level of one storey between them.

The western front of the house (the part we can't see) was built 1725-1735, the eastern front (the part we can) being begun in 1734. They were both built for the same man: the first Marquess of Rockingham, who had come into the property in 1723 and who died in 1750. The east façade was designed by Flitcroft (who designed Hoober Stand) and altered by John Carr in 1782-4. His work is reflected in the giant Corinthian columns and three bay pediments. Carr's great achievement however, is the magnificent stable block

of 1758, which was built on a scale almost as lavish as the house!
Fifteen bays surround a great courtyard with a central fountain, the
whole thing being surmounted by a domed clocktower - a truly
magnificent piece of architecture.

Wentworth Woodhouse is both inspiring and sad. Though not
actually ruinous or totally empty there is an air of decay, of neglect.
Perhaps it is the smoke blackening of the Industrial Revolution that
has created this atmosphere. Until recently Wentworth Woodhouse
was the home of the Lady Mabel College of Physical Education, but
now the whole range of college buildings stand empty. (These
include a swimming pool, a students union block and modern halls
of residence.)

*From Wentworth Woodhouse follow the driveway to the main road,
cross it and proceed down Clayfolds Lane passing the pretty and castellated
Round House on the right, looking like a sawn off windmill or a giant
child's sandcastle. (A similar building may be found at an estate farmhouse
by the road out of Wentworth.) Our route avoids the heart of the village,
and instead turns right by the former Methodist Chapel, following a
footpath signed to Elsecar. Ascend the field to a hedge, and then bear left,
passing through a succession of stiles before reaching a further footpath
sign at a junction of routes. Ignore a track leading off left towards
Wentworth's churches, and bear right downhill, then left, to yet another
footpath sign. At a stile turn right, following a path up the hillside towards
King's Wood. At the next stile ignore a path going straight up towards
trees and bear left, then right to a stile at the entrance to King's Wood. Pass
through King's Wood, then cross a field beyond to reach the start of the walk
at Elsecar - a fine end to a fine ramble.*

10: WENTWORTH WOODHOUSE -
Keppel's Column

Two interesting churches, a beheaded earl, a displaced Chinaman,
a grotto in lovely gardens, woods, lakes, cornfields and a monument
to a disgraced admiral are all to be found on this, our second visit
to the follies of Wentworth Woodhouse. Two playgrounds, along
with lots of woodlands and open spaces make this a good walk for
the kids, but don't work them too hard: this is a "fair ramble".

Getting there:	Leave the M1 at junction 36. Follow the A6135 through Hoyland Common and beyond Tankersley Park turn left onto the lane to Wentworth. Park in the village car park by play area and cricket ground.
Distance:	6 miles approx.
Map ref:	SK 388 982 Landranger 111
Rating:	Walk *** Follies & General Interest ***

So here we are again back in the village of Wentworth as promised!
Our previous walk skirted the edge of Wentworth on the way back
to Elsecar, but on this occasion we have time to explore the village
at our leisure.

Turning right out of the car park by Wentworth Cricket Club we
proceed along the main village street towards that hub of all rural
communities: the church or in this case the churches, for Wentworth
has two - one grand and Victorian and the other small and ruined.
The Old Church is now disused. A notice informs us that "This
ancient church is maintained by the Redundant Churches Fund".
The nave has gone and the tower is ruinous but the mediaeval
chancel and north chapel remain as the Wentworth Chapel.
Externally the structure is predominantly seventeenth century, but
still retains vestiges of the earlier church. Stone bought by Thomas
Wentworth from the sale of Monk Bretton Priory after the Dissolution
is said to be incorporated into the fabric of the building.

The main attraction of the old church is its monuments. Keys can

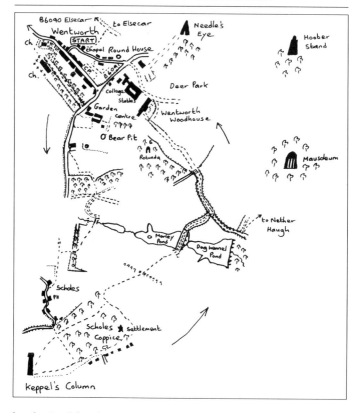

be obtained for closer inspection if required, but much can be seen by simply looking through the window. One alabaster monument to the Gascoyne family dates from 1460, but by far the most striking is the colourful monument to Sir William Wentworth with its kneeling figures, dating from 1612. Next door to it, kneeling in a niche in the wall, is the somewhat flamboyant effigy of Thomas Wentworth, the first Earl of Strafford. The inscription reads:

Thomas Wentworth
Earl of Strafforde, Visfcount Wentworth,
Baron Wentworth of Wentworth Woodhouse

Newmarch Oversley and Raby .
Lord Lieutenant of Ireland, Lord President of the North of England
and Knight of the most noble Order of the Garter.
His birth was upon Good Friday the 13th April 1593 his death
upon the 12th of May 1641. His soule through the mercy
of God lives in eternal bli*ffe* and his memory shall
never die in these Kingdomes.

The monument tactfully makes no mention of the fact that
Wentworth's demise was occasioned by the fall of the headsman's
axe, for here, in this tiny Yorkshire church, repose (so we are told!)
the mortal remains of one who played out a tragic role on the fateful
stage of Stuart history! The story of Wentworth's rise and subsequent
fall from grace is reminiscent of the classical tragedy of Sejanus.
Overly privileged and high handed - yes, lining his pockets -
possibly, but Strafford was in no way guilty of the charge of high
treason which was levelled at him by a spiteful and venomous
Parliament which howled for his blood. Lodged in the Tower and
subsequently tried before the Lords, Strafford fought desperately
for his life, and put up such a noble defence that he emerged
guiltless. It did not save him. Thwarted, Pym and the Commons
resorted to less noble means, a tyrannous Act of Attainder, which
only needed the threat of war and insurrection to force a reluctant
Charles I to sign his trusted servant's death warrant. Anxious for the
safety of his threatened queen and hoping to win peace for his
troubled kingdom Charles gave assent to the Act (Strafford having
bravely written a letter releasing the king from his promise to
protect his life and fortune). Charles never forgave himself. His
most trusted advisor went to the scaffold and the stage was set for
the final act of the tragedy that led to Civil War and Charles's own
eventual appointment with the headsman.

Thomas Wentworth came from an influential family. (He took
the title of Strafford, incidentally, from the name of the local
wapentake). Thomas's father, Sir William, was Sheriff of Yorkshire
1601-2 and was created Baronet in 1611. With an estate worth £6000
per annum he was the wealthiest gentleman in Yorkshire. Strafford
lived in no meaner style. It is recorded that his grand household at
Wentworth Woodhouse consisted of 64 persons, 49 of them servants.

In the churchyard there are monuments to less illustrious but no less interesting denizens of bygone Wentworth. The northern section of the churchyard is dominated by the massive Fitzwilliam Vault, and to the east of the main path is a gravestone bearing the following curious inscription:

TO THE MEMORY OF

閣荒勵

CHOW KWANG TSEAY
A NATIVE OF CHINHAE NEAR NINGPO CHINA
BETTER KNOWN BY THE ENGLISH NAMES OF
JOHN DENNIS BLONDE
WHO WAS BAPTISED IN WENTWORTH CHURCH ON
SUNDAY OCTOBER 15TH 1848, AND DIED AT ASHCROFT
IN THIS PARISH FEBY.6TH 1850, AGED 17 YRS
AND WAS BURIED NEAR THIS SPOT.

Therein lies a tale! Chow Kwang Tseay came to live in Wentworth when he was ten years old. His origins are obscure. Certainly he was taken from Ningpo on a British warship bound for India, but how he came to be on the ship is uncertain. Was he sold by his parents? kidnapped? a cabin boy? a stowaway? We can only speculate. The boy was befriended by a merchant by the name of Captain Forster, who appears to have originated from the Wentworth area, and it was to him that "Little Chopsticks" owed his subsequent good fortune.

The 5th Earl Fitzwilliam was apparently persuaded by Forster to undertake the care and education of the boy, and he was duly placed in the Ashcroft Academy under the tuition of Mr William Beardsall. When he was baptized at Wentworth he adopted the name John Dennis Blonde, taking his surname from the Warship on which he had sailed: HMS Blondi. At the Academy Chow Kwang Tseay began to grow into a young man, but the vexing question of his future employment was suddenly and tragically resolved by his untimely death at the age of 17. He was given a good send off locally and here he now slumbers, far from his native land.

A short walk from the Old Church is the New. Holy Trinity was built 1875-7 and designed by J.L.Pearson. It is a magnificent thirteenth-century style Gothic church with transepts, a tall spire and graceful lines. This is the soaring, solid church of the Victorian

Fitzwilliams.

From the church a tree lined avenue leads towards Wentworth Woodhouse Park, passing behind the village to an iron gate. Cross the road to the Wentworth Garden Centre, and bear left, passing a landscaped car park, craft shops and children's adventure playground. A right turn leads past the tree nursery into a restored nineteenth-century Japanese ornamental garden with ponds, stepping stones, decaying statues, and most interestingly of all, our first folly, The Bear Pit.

The entrances to The Bear Pit are essentially fragments of the original seventeenth-century house of the Earl of Strafford grafted onto an eighteenth-century grotto. A short tunnel leads into a room with barred niches where the bears were (allegedly!) kept. A spiral stair with iron railings leads up to a terrace behind the garden. One can easily imagine the faltering steps of the gentlemen and the nervous giggles of the ladies who first ventured into this Arcadian catacomb at the urging of their host. The entrances, however, offer the most fascination, belonging as they do to an earlier period. The style is mannerist, c.1630, being decorated with volutes, festoons and shields. One can only guess at the appearance of the fine house to which they once belonged.

Retrace your steps through the garden centre to the road, turn left, and follow it for some distance until a lodge house with a fine classical portico appears on the left. Pass through a stile by the gate and follow a footpath diagonally across wheatfields, noting the fine rotunda with a statue in Wentworth Woodhouse Park on the left. On reaching a gate and stile at the woodland perimeter continue onwards along a narrow corridor between trees to arrive at another gate and stile by a track. Continue onwards across yet another arable field to a gate and an elegant bridge at the start of the first of Wentworth Woodhouse's ornamental lakes. Polluted water plunges over a sudsy weir. The Marquess would not have approved!

Beyond the bridge bear right then left, along the field edge by a plantation. Half way along, pass through the trees by a ruin (overgrown) beyond which an elusive stile gives access to the pasture. Ascend the pasture to a gate and pass alongside the field boundary, turning right beyond outbuildings to meet the metalled road by Red House Farm.

On entering the lane turn left and follow it downhill as it meanders through the village of Scholes, passing the Bay Horse and Scholes Cricket Club on the left. Beyond Scholes, where the road veers sharply to the right up the hill, continue onwards into woodland. A short distance on and a path leads off to the right, crossing a small footbridge to emerge onto open common. From here a well defined footpath, occasionally criss-crossed by drainage channels, leads up the hillside to Keppel's Column.

Keppel's Column is a folly in the grand style. Basically it is a single, solitary Tuscan column upon a hill, but did you ever see a Tuscan column 115 feet high with an internal staircase, windows and a viewing platform on the top? Architecturally speaking it is a gigantic absurdity, but if you are a connoisseur of dubious taste and architectural ugliness you will instantly realise that you are standing before the work of a master.

That master was John Carr, and his employer was the second Marquess of Rockingham, who in 1778 was obviously intent on matching the architectural paranoia of his predecessor, the first Marquess. Built to rival Hoober Stand on the hillside opposite, Keppel's Column was (ostensibly!) erected as a monument to Viscount Keppel, Ist Lord of the Admiralty during Rockingham's government ministry. Keppel seems hardly worthy of such a singular honour. The monument in fact commemorates his acquittal after being court-martialled on charges of incompetence and "scandalous haste in quitting the scene of a naval engagement" at the Battle of Ushant. Rockingham was Keppel's friend, and believed that Keppel was actually just a scapegoat for the misdemeanours of Tory politicians who had been embezzling funds intended for the upkeep of the Navy. Be this as it may, it is a lame excuse, if ever there was one, for building such a monument as this. One feels that it was more of a pretext than a justification.

The base of the column is vandalised, which no doubt explains why the entrance has been walled up. This is a pity, as the thing you want to do most with such a structure is to admire the view from the top (which is, after all, the reason why it was built). The Wainhouse Tower in Halifax and the Jubilee Tower in Huddersfield are kept locked, but are both open to the public on Bank Holiday weekends, briefly becoming tourist attractions. The admission fee to these follies contributes towards keeping them in good repair, and it is sad that no such plans are envisaged for Keppel's Column and Hoober Stand, both of which are structures intended to draw the eye and excite interest.

From Keppel's Column follow the well defined footpath back to Scholes Coppice. (Bell ground - all the woods around here were planted to obscure early mine workings.) On reaching the woodland (and a labyrinth of paths) bear left, following a well defined path along the edge of the coppice until another (equally) well defined route leads off to the right down the wood. At the far end of the plantation ignore the stile into the pasture and turn left, following a path which leads below the steep bank of an arable field. On reaching a small footbridge bear right to the edge of an another field and then follow a well defined path which leads across two arable fields before finally descending to the dam across Dog Kennel Pond. Cross the dam and follow the track up the hillside to join the Hoober Stand route, walked previously, coming in from the right. Turn left up to the deer park and the magnificent southern front of the Wentworth Woodhouse mansion. Pass to right of the mansion and stable blocks and leave the park. On reaching the road cross to Clayfield Lane and continue onwards to the cricket field, passing The Round House on the right. Cross the playground and football field to the car park.

The Round House, Wentworth Woodhouse. (walks 9 & 10)

North Riding

11: SORRELSYKES PARK AND THE AYSGARTH "ROCKET"

A pretty Dales village, a waterfall, a ruined church and an odd concentration of highly individual follies characterise this fine promenade along the limestone terraces of Wensleydale, not far from the famous Aysgarth Falls.

Getting there:	Leave the A1 at Leeming Bar and follow the A684 to Leyburn. (Alternatively the A6108 to Leyburn from Ripon, via Masham.) Continue along the A684 towards Aysgarth. Just beyond Swinithwaite turn left onto the B6160 to West Burton. Note: West Burton may also be approached from Langstrothdale via Kettlewell and Buckden (B6160), or from Ingleton via Ribblehead, Hawes and Bainbridge (B6255-A684) - both highly scenic routes.
Distance:	4 miles. Easy, kids will enjoy it, but take care on the busy A684.
Map ref:	SE 017 866 Landranger 98
Rating:	Walk *** Follies & General Interest ***

> Before you know a stranger you must summer him
> and winter him and summer him again
>
> *Old Yorkshire saying*

Limestone at last! Waterfalls, ravines, clints, grykes, and caves characterise the distinctive landscape of the Yorkshire Dales National Park. The valley of the Ure was carved out by glaciers, and when they receded they left behind the beginnings of today's unique landscape. The white scars and velvet turf of the limestone terraces

Mowbray Castle, Hackfall

Fisher's Hall, Hackfali

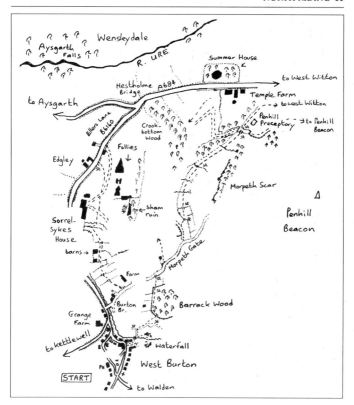

are a walker's paradise, which with ascent give way to heathery moors and gritstone outcrops. The predominantly rural nature of the Dales has also left a rich historical legacy. Lynchets, prehistoric hut circles and ancient earthworks abound, undisturbed by the passage of centuries. The Yoredale Series limestone around Wensleydale is scarred and honeycombed with the remains of intensive lead mining activity. Today the mines are derelict and the tough hardbitten miners who once worked them not even a memory.

This is "Herriot Country", but you will search in vain for those poverty stricken hill farmers who comprised the bulk of his

97

customers. Since the war the history of the Dales has been one of steady depopulation. Poverty, unemployment (and more recently the soaring prices of property) have forced the genuine dalesman to leave his birthright and to live in the towns to the north and south. He has been supplanted by the TV producer, the yuppie accountant and the "off comed 'un" who will pay a king's ransom for a converted barn or a weekend cottage in a Dales village. Consequently the only "true born" dalesfolk who remain are those who were always well heeled, or old folk who had homes here before the Dales became fashionable. On a summer weekend you will find the villages of the Dales jammed up with walkers, climbers, cavers and tourists, but come here on a January Wednesday and you will find ghost towns filled with affluent, trendily modernised and quite empty properties.

West Burton slumbers peacefully around its greens, tucked away in the folds of Yoredale's shattered landscape. Geographically it suffers from an identity crisis. Standing near the meeting of Bishopdale and Waldendale not far from the point where both of these tributaries join the the Ure in Wensleydale, it is perhaps more to be associated with the two former than the latter. The confusion is by no means new. The village in past times has been variously known as Burton-in-Bishopdale and Burton-cum-Walden. West Burton was once an industrial community of hand knitters, dyers and woolcombers. Today it exhibits the imported affluence typical of all dales villages. Central to West Burton is its magnificent village cross, like a miniature church spire standing on a flight of steps. The cross was erected in 1820 and restored in 1889.

The village stocks stand adjacent. Though obviously not the original ones they have nevertheless an interesting record of use. In the seventeenth century Quakerism spread throughout the Dales, and was not always well received. In 1660 Samuel Watson of Stainforth Hall in Ribblesdale came to West Burton with the intention of holding a Friends meeting. Unfortunately "One wicked fellow with a great staff and pistol" threatened to shoot him, and beat him unconscious with his staff. Poor Watson was revived, put in the stocks for a while and eventually thrown in the river. So much for Dales hospitality!

Our walk starts by the West Burton Methodist Chapel. Follow the road

Cross,
West
Burton

through the village, passing swings, the village cross and stocks. To the east of the village where the road winds to the left, turn right, following a signed route "To Waterfall", passing the old mill to a footbridge over the beck just downstream of West Burton's fine cataract, a place for a picnic or a paddle! From the footbridge our route proceeds via Barrack Wood to Morpeth (or Morphet) Gate. This is an old drove road; the word "Gate" has not the modern meaning but is derived from the Norse "Gata" meaning "road", or "way". This was originally the main highway up Wensleydale from Middleham, passing over West Witton Moor beneath the flanks of Penhill Beacon. Once this remote trackway was alive with traffic heading for Yoredale's markets and fairs, today it is frequented only by its memories and the occasional party of hikers.

At Morpeth Gate turn right, following the lane uphill until a sign (to Templar's Chapel) appears on the left. From here a straightforward route leads around the hillside along a grassy limestone terrace, from which there are fine views to Castle Bolton and Addleborough. Soon we reach a stile in a wall entering a lane, on the far side of which lies the fenced ruins of the Penhill Preceptory.

The notice reveals all and nothing: "Penhill Preceptory - These walls and graves belong to a chapel in a preceptory of the Knights Templars, built in c.1200 and handed over, on their suppression in 1312 to the Hospitallers. The chapel, the remains of which were uncovered in 1840, served adjoining residential buildings that have not been exposed."

The Templars, along with their arch rivals the Hospitallers, or Knights of St John, were religious orders of knights of great military prowess who had taken priestly vows of poverty, chastity and obedience. The origins of these military orders of soldier/monks lay in Outremer, "The Land beyond the Sea", which was the mediaeval name for the Holy Land at the time of the Crusades. According to the Frankish historian Guillaume De Tyre, the Order of the Poor Knights of Christ and the Temple of Solomon was founded in 1118 by one Hugues De Payen, a vassal of the Count of Champagne. According to legend, De Payen, with eight comrades at his side, presented himself to King Baudoin I of Jerusalem (whose elder brother Godfroi De Bouillon had captured the Holy City nineteen years previously). The declared purpose of the Templars was to protect the highways leading to Jerusalem in order to ensure the safety of pilgrims en-route to the Holy Sepulchre. Baudoin was so pleased with this noble objective that he placed a wing of the royal palace at their disposal. According to tradition, their quarters were built on the site of the ancient Temple of Solomon, and it was from this that the order was to derive its name.

From such humble beginnings the order grew to fame and fortune, and by the middle of the twelfth century they had established bases all over Europe. In 1128 their Constitution was drawn up by St Bernard of Clairvaux, and with such powerful support their influence and numbers grew accordingly. Scott's "Ivanhoe" gives us a good description of a Templar. Haughty and arrogant he wore (as his Rule dictated) a long beard and a mantle of white linen with a distinctive red cross. Often Templars might be seen as advisors to princes and kings.

With the fall of Jerusalem to the Saracens the Templars set up their headquarters first in Cyprus and then in France. Under papal authority they enjoyed exemption from taxes, tithes and interdict, becoming as a result increasingly powerful, wealthy and arrogant. From their traditional stamping grounds in Palestine their sphere of influence became increasingly the political arena of mediaeval Europe.

The Templars were essentially a secret society. Ruled over by a Grand Master, their rites and inner mysteries were known only to initiates of the brotherhood. Unfortunately this deliberate veil of secrecy created not only a tightly knit brotherhood but also a fertile seeding ground for the accusations of their enemies. In 1307, supported by Pope Clement IV, Philip the Fair of France (who had long cast covetous eyes on the Templars' vast assets) accused the Templars of heresy and witchcraft. Arrests were made and "confessions" extracted by torture. The Templars were said to have worshipped a Devil called Baphomet, a bearded head, which had given them occult powers. There were charges of homosexuality and obscene rites. The outcome was never in doubt; between 1307 and 1314 hundreds of Templars were burnt at the stake, their assets confiscated and the Order scattered. In March 1314, the Order's Grand Master, Jacques De Molay, was roasted to death over a slow fire. The Templars had passed into the obscurity of history.

In England the Templars fared better. Philip's own son-in-law, Edward II of England at first rallied to the Order's defence, but was eventually persuaded to suppress them. In the scramble to get hold of their assets some Templars were arrested, and it is reported that John De Bellerby, Master of the Penhill Preceptory, was imprisoned with others in York Castle in 1309. The majority, however, were simply ejected from their preceptories, which were handed over to the Hospitallers and we must assume that their ultimate fate was considerably less unpleasant than that of their European brethren.

The Penhill Preceptory was excavated by Mr Anderson of

Swinithwaite Hall, who found spurs and fragments of armour. Prior to this it had been just a mysterious mound. Preceptory churches are unusual in that they were circular in plan. The Penhill Preceptory is even more unusual in that it is not. The outline is of a rectangular building with a door at one end and a small chancel at the other. In front of the chancel lie three stone coffins the size of which makes us marvel at the smallness of our mediaeval ancestors. It must have been a tight fit for a dead knight!!

After inspecting the Templars chapel, retrace your steps to the lane and then turn right, following it down to the road by Temple Farm, which reputedly stands on the site of the Preceptory's secular buildings, and opposite, where our path joins the main road, we encounter the first folly on our walk. Surrounded by a high wall amidst an overgrown garden, a dilapidated summer house stands on a small knoll. This summer house belonged to Swinithwaite Hall, a mile down the road, being built in 1792 for Mr T.J. Anderson. The architect was John Foss, of Richmond. The building has an octagonal base with a fine bas relief of a pointer above the door. Inside, a staircase leads to a domed octagonal chamber, which apparently still possesses most of its fine plasterwork. A balcony runs around the outside. Lonely and neglected, the traffic to Aysgarth rumbles by and the building stands forlorn.

Turn left, and follow the main road (A684) downhill to its junction with Ellers Lane (B6160). Turn left down this road, with the follies now in view on the left.

The Sorrelsykes Follies were to all intents and purposes built as eyecatchers for Sorrelsykes Farm opposite, which (on this side at least) displays the frontage of an eighteenth-century Palladian mansion. There are three follies standing in a neat row on the edge of the limestone terrace, in company with a typical dales barn. The first and largest, known locally as the "Rocket Ship" is essentially a cone rising from a square base with a small room inside. The folly is built of local limestone, in a style which suggests that its anonymous builder was more used to constructing lead mine adits than fanciful follies. In true lead miner fashion it seems he decided that the cone might become unsafe, and so "propped" it with a series of buttresses. As a result the whole thing looks like something out of a Dan Dare cartoon. It was constructed around 1860. The second folly is less impressive, being little more than a small gateway constructed from two cones with an arch in between. Finally we come to the Pepper Pot. With a large smoke hole, this odd, spinning top like structure was reputedly built around 1921, and was used for the curing of bacon!

The final folly in the Sorrelsykes Group is a sham ruin. This lies beyond the barn, just below the edge of the next limestone terrace. Standing above a steep rocky scree and half hidden by the trees, this eyecatcher was apparently built to obscure the remains of eighteenth-century lead workings. Traces of the mine may still be seen where an old gully leads down to the last vestiges of the spoil heaps. The main part of the ruin consists of a blank arch, an *oeil-de-boeuf* window and a small classical pediment. One suspects that today it is more ruinous than when it was first constructed.

And so our walk proceeds by quaint barns back to Morpeth Gate, passing Sorrelsykes House on the right, and following a well defined route, which, after a passing a succession of barns and stiles finally emerges into Morpeth Gate near Flanders Hall. Turn right and follow the lane, which crosses the Little Beck by the picturesque Burton Bridge and rejoins the B6160 opposite Grange Farm Cottage. Turn left, and follow the lane through West Burton back to the start of our walk, passing Peel House on the right. If you have time you can revisit the waterfall, or even drive to the nearby Aysgarth Falls. A fine end to a pleasant ramble.

12: THE DRUID'S TEMPLE

This short but pleasant walk features moors, conifers, fine views and the mysterious standing stones of Yorkshire's own "Stonehenge": a nineteenth-century folly which some people confuse with the real thing!

Getting there:	The Druid's Temple is well off the beaten track. From Ripon follow the A6108 to Masham via Lightwater Valley and West Tanfield. From Masham a minor road (signed) leads past Swinton Park, heading south-west to Ilton. Beyond Ilton, continue onwards towards Healey. The road first descends to the Sole Beck via a series of bends, then runs straight uphill for a short distance. On the left a No Through Road sign marks the end of Knowle Lane. Following the signs, proceed along Knowle Lane (avoiding local fauna) to the car park and picnic area in the Druid's Plantation.
Distance:	3¹/₂ miles. Easy! Make sure you take the kids, they'll love it!!
Map ref:	SE 175 787 Landranger 99
Rating:	Walk * Folly ***

As a walk this is a bit of a disappointment, but as a folly it must not be missed! The countryside around Ilton is attractive enough, being a slice of that rather obscure and unspectacular (but quite unspoilt) landscape which lies between the Yorkshire Dales National Park and the fertile Vale of Mowbray. It is characterised by upland pastures, sleepy little villages, coniferous forestry and gently rolling shooting moors. Here are the "fringe" Dales, undramatic but also untouristified. Forestry, farming, gamekeeping and drinking water are the preoccupations of most folks hereabouts. The only snag is that in consequence of these activities the would-be-rambler finds his scope severely curtailed. On the hills around Ilton we are in the

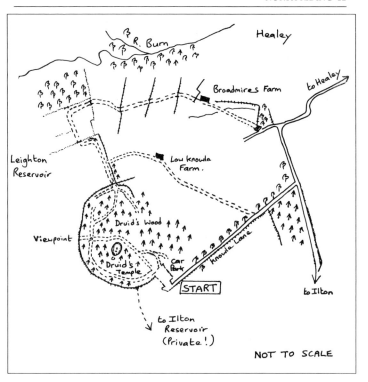

land of "Private - Keep Out".

The Druid's Temple is public enough: the fine car park and picnic area positively invites the visitor to come and explore.

From the picnic site/car park ignore obvious routes leading into the plantation and instead proceed back down Knowle Lane (the access road). At the T-junction, turn left, and when the road turns right towards Healey, turn left again, following the signed access road to Broadmires Farm. Passing Broadmires Farm on the right, continue onwards, following a track through a succession of gates. Beyond the fifth gate, by a plantation (on right) the track leads left up the hillside to another gate, then winds up the hill, passing gate and track leading to Low Knowle Farm on the left. Continue onwards to a gate leading into Druid's Plantation.

On any summer's evening at Ilton you will find hundreds of wild rabbits frolicking by the roadside, but unfortunately cars outnumber them and the steady tramp down Knowle Lane is on a virtual carpet of small, furry, flattened corpses. The whole area teems with other wildlife as well: hedgehogs, squirrels, pheasants, curlews all abound in this countryside.

Ascending the hillside near Low Knowle Farm there are fine views across the Vale of Mowbray to the Cleveland and Hambleton Hills before we finally enter the all-obscuring conifers of Druids Wood. In the forest, ignore a path leading off right along the forest boundary and continue onwards 100 yards or so to a fork in the track. Turn right, and follow the track round to the left to reach an imitation dolmen at a crossing of routes. This is the Viewpoint, where a gap has been left in the forest to offer views over Leighton Reservoir (which supplies Leeds), along with views of Colsterdale and Great Haw. From here another left turn leads unerringly to the centrepiece of our walk - the Druid's Temple.

The Druid's Temple is a place to let your imagination run riot. Here is Yorkshire's own "Stonehenge", hidden deep in the conifers. Strangely enough, it is not a circle, being oval in shape - but its purpose is obvious - the sacrifice of small children, especially naughty small children! Some people have been fooled by the monument, believing it to be "the real thing" but no-one with any knowledge of genuine megalithic sites would be taken in. An attached plan and notice by the entrance reveals all:

'PLAN OF DRUID'S TEMPLE'
A replica built about 1820 to a design by Mr. Danby.
based on an original plan by P.T. Runton Esq.

William Danby (1752-1833), the eccentric squire of Swinton Hall, when not crenellating his home into a "castle", fancied himself as a bit of a philosopher, writing such tracts as *Travelling Thoughts* and *Thoughts on Various Subjects* which were published a year before his death. Perhaps his philosophy was the inspiration behind the opening of his parklands "for public inspection" and his efforts to relieve unemployment in the area. The Temple was built as a result of one such effort, and one marvels at what the unemployed labourers who toiled to create this chaotic confusion of bogus dolmens, menhirs and phallic standing stones must have thought of

The Druid's Temple

their task, which, considering the size of some of the "sarsens" which had to be transported to this remote site, was no mean achievement! Even if versed in the terminology of megalithic antiquity they would have found the project bizarre, but lacking any such knowledge they must have thought that "T'owd squire" had gone soft in the head! As he was paying the wages and providing welcome employment however, they would no doubt have gone along with the idea and spun out the job for as long as possible.

Stone circles are places of mystery and legend, and even bogus ones are no exception. One local guidebook (no doubt seeking increased sales) claims that Danby offered to provide food, and a subsequent annuity to anyone who was prepared to live as a hermit in the temple for seven years. The would-be-hermit was to speak to no-one and to allow his beard and hair to grow. One man reputedly eked out this arduous existence for $4^1/2$ years before giving in to the bleak Pennine climate. The story (despite continuing reports of disappearing picnic hampers in the Masham district) is almost certainly apocryphal.

From the Druid's Temple an obvious route leads within a few hundred yards back to the car park/picnic site, where we can sit and relax awhile, after a short but most interesting perambulation.

The Swinton Estate did not remain in the hands of the Danbys. After the death of the old squire at the age of 81 (which was much lamented as Danby had been a benevolent and considerate landlord), Swinton Castle and its parklands were acquired by wool magnate Samuel Cunliffe Lister, the first Lord Masham. Lord Masham set out to complete the work of the Danbys by enlarging the park, but he was no folly builder and never managed to surpass the ingenuity and imagination of his predecessor. Squire Danby may sleep in a quite forgotten grave, but here, his most striking monument, surrounded by a "sacred grove" of gloomy Forestry Commission conifers, will ensure that his memory remains (like the trees) quite evergreen.

13: THE HACKFALL FOLLIES

Remote, neglected and indescribably peaceful, where the Ure flows through a rocky gorge surrounded by dense overgrown woodlands, this walk features a pleasant village, fine views across to the Cleveland Hills, river scenery and three very important (yet little known) follies.

Getting there:	From Pateley Bridge follow the B6265 towards Ripon and turn off left, following unclassified road to Kirkby Malzeard. From Kirkby Malzeard follow signs to Grewelthorpe. From Ripon leave by the Pateley Bridge road and the first turning off to the right leads directly to Grewelthorpe. Steep crags, and (in summer) dense undergrowth, make this walk not really suitable for small children.
Distance:	5 miles approx.
Map ref:	SE 229 765 Landranger 99
Rating:	Walk *** Follies & General Interest ***

> To Hackfall's calm retreats, where nature reigns,
> in rural pride transported fancy flies.
> Oh! bear me, Goddess to those sylvan plains,
> where all around unlaboured beauties rise....
> *1822 Guidebook*

Hackfall is a surprise. Its existence is quite unsuspected by anyone passing through the area, and its follies are elusive. The area is quite off the beaten track - getting your car to Grewelthorpe is by itself a feat of navigation! I came here on a hot Saturday in August and walked for six hours without seeing another human being! At first there is a pleasant village with a duckpond, happy pastures and views over the Vale of Mowbray to the distant Kilburn White Horse, but on entering the woods at Mickley Barras I found myself entering another world: overgrown, forgotten and haunted, a place left

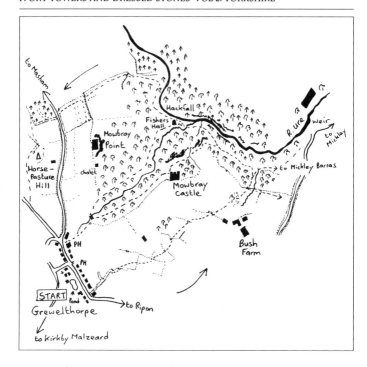

alone with its memories.

Our journey to Hackfall starts from Grewelthorpe village pond, following the road towards Ripon. A short distance on turn left (footpath signed To Mickley) passing through a gate to follow a grassy track between hedges. Pass through another gate and continue onwards, ignoring the waymarked lane which joins on the left. Beyond a ruin (on the right), the lane ends at a gate by a holly tree. Pass over a stile (on the right) and follow the hedge round to a second waymarked stile in the field corner. Entering the field, bear slightly to the right (following the same line of travel) and cross to the next stile, 70 yards up from the bottom right hand corner of the field. Continue in the same direction to the next stile (waymarked) then across the next field to a post stile, which enters (at the time of writing) a field of sugar beet. Head towards trees, to the right of which will be found *a stile and a gate. Continue onwards to the next stile passing Bush Farm on the right, and then after passing a solitary tree at the top of a slope descend steeply down to a waymarked gate which leads into woodlands.*

Proceed into the woods, ignoring a descending path on the right, and follow an overgrown path left around the hillside until it joins a rather more well used path coming in from the right. This path leads towards Hackfall Woods.

Hackfall is a place of memories. The first echo of them appears, when in the midst of dense woodland we discover overgrown steps passing up through the crags. At Mowbray Castle the echoes resonate still louder, but it is not until we stand in the midst of the ruined octagonal pavilion of Fisher's Hall, looking at the glinting fragments of glass and shells in the walls, that something sad and long vanished crowds in upon your fleeting human presence and pleads with you to share its story.

The story begins with a tablet over the Gothick doorway of Fisher's Hall, which bears the inscription "W. A. 1750". Give these "bones" flesh and we see William Aislabie, plans and designs in hand, exploring the woods, pointing excitedly here and there, surrounded by the nodding assent of his gardeners. Aislabie had recently discovered this steep and remote section of the Ure Valley, and for him it was the ideal place to develop into a "Romantick" garden. The Aislabies were gardeners and folly builders extraordinaire. William's father, John, had created the beautiful gardens at Studley Royal, and the young William, rightly recognising them to be a masterpiece, had decided, rather than disturb his father's work, to develop his ideas and interests elsewhere. Searching for a suitable place he had discovered Hackfall, and his prayers had been answered.

Work began at Hackfall in 1750 and the end result of all the labour was the first (and possibly the finest) "Romantick" garden in all England. The "Hanging Woods", sheer cliffs and turbulent river more than fulfilled the fashionable eighteenth-century whimsy for romantick "Arcadian" landscapes filled with nymphs and satyrs. Where today is "The Fountain Plain" based on designs from Langley's *New Principles of Gardening* (1728)? Once, in the midst of a now stagnant pond, a fountain threw water to a great height; and nearby, a "cascade" fell over 40 feet by a grotto and a rustic temple made from great boulders. The Hackfall Gardens were a wonder, and people came from miles around to see them, including such famous eighteenth-century travellers as Arthur Young and William Gilpin.

The nineteenth century too viewed Hackfall with wonder. In Victorian times it was owned by Lord Ripon, and a broken obelisk (if you can find it) dates from this period. Hackfall was a pleasant day's excursion for those taking the waters in Harrogate, and in Thorpe's *Illustrated Guide* to Harrogate of 1886 regular day trips to the "Hackfall Gardens" are advertised. Even at the turn of the twentieth century Hackfall was a favourite resort, would-be-tourists paying a small fee for access to the grounds and gardens. The 1930s saw the gardens in decay and today, apart from the half hidden ruins of the follies, there is virtually no trace of their former glory. The wheel has turned full circle, and now Hackfall is in much the same condition as it must have been on that day in 1750 when William Aislabie first discovered the place. The woods, the rocks and the river remain, a stern example of how quickly nature can erase the traces of man and his works, and only the crumbling follies in their midst, left alone with their memories, offer any hint of the days when this forsaken place was one of Yorkshire's chief resorts, the Victorian equivalent of nearby Lightwater Valley.

Perhaps in winter, the traces of Hackfall's former glories are easier to find, but this is not so in summer when the vegetation chokes everything, and creates an atmosphere of green claustrophobia. The woods seem full of sounds, none of them human. By the rapids of the Ure we might well be in the great forests of the untamed American wilderness!

The walk in this book visits Hackfall's three major follies. There is more, but to get a comprehensive picture of what Hackfall must have been like would take a number of visits. *The routes from the village to the woods are all on public rights of way, but the paths around Hackfall itself are of less certain legality, and arduous to follow in parts. They are, for the most part, marked by purple paint spots on the trees, which does at least imply that it is intended to be some sort of a nature trail.*

Entering Hackfall Woods directions are as follows: when the path starts to descend towards the River Ure, look for a small (not obvious) path which leads up through crags via a series of stone steps. The path leads precariously around the top of the crags, passing above a magnificent deep cleft on the right. After bearing slightly left to cross a small stream at the top of the wood, continue around the hillside until Mowbray Castle appears on the left.

Perched on the crags which form the natural boundaries of the estate, Mowbray Castle towers over woods and river. The view of it from across the valley was painted by Turner in 1816. The Castle is basically a sham ruined "shell keep" faintly reminiscent of the rather more genuine Multangular Tower in York. The detail is excellent. Even inside we are led to believe that we are looking at the ruin of what was once a floored and roofed building! This of course is quite untrue, for Mowbray Castle was built as a ruin! Aislabie named his castle after the De Mowbrays, feudal knights who once held vast estates and forests in the area. Aislabie's choice of name was therefore not only apt and "romantick" but was also no doubt intended to lend a touch of authenticity to his spurious and whimsical creation.

From Mowbray Castle continue onwards (following purple marks on trees!) until the top of the ravine is reached. Resisting the highly visible temptations of the Hackfall Inn, which can be seen over the fields, turn right, cross the stream and then follow the path down the far side of the ravine. After a short ascent to join another path, the path leads down towards the river. Bear right by a fallen tree to emerge at the ruined pavilion of Fisher's Hall which stands forlornly on a knoll above the River Ure.

Fisher's Hall was not built as a ruin. Neglect and vandalism have given it its present appearance. Once upon a time this octagonal lancet windowed pavilion was a grotto room, its walls lined with coloured glass and shells.(A good example of what it must have been like can be seen in the "Shell Room" in the gatehouse of Skipton Castle.) Fisher's Hall was named after John Aislabie's chief gardener who, up to his death in 1743 also worked for the son William. Fisher's Hall was not sited here by accident. Below, where the River Ure rushes beneath steep crags and overhanging trees, the gorge is at its most beautiful.

From Fisher's Hall descend steps to the riverside path and turn left. Soon a sandy beach appears on the right with the remains of campfires. Beyond it a path ascends through woods up Limehouse Hill to meet a wall with a coniferous plantation beyond. Bear left, following a wall up to a gate at the edge of the wood. From here an indistinct path leads up pastures (wall, fence and ditch on right), to another gate, and another pasture, beyond which lies the road.

In the final pasture before entering the road a track (not a right of way) leads off left to a gate beyond which the edge of the wood may be followed in order to inspect the magnificent folly of Mowbray Point. (If you do not wish to trespass the folly may be seen distantly from the top of Horsepasture Hill.)

Mowbray Point is in a sad state. Its rafters have collapsed, and its wall niches and ornate plasterwork are shattered beyond repair. Enough remains, however, to give you some idea of the interior, and the outside walls are still in their original (contrivedly ruined) condition. Mowbray Point was built as a banqueting house, and it was here that the Victorian tourists would stop to take tea, and no doubt have a rest after the arduous climb up from the river.

It is a two faced building. The side facing the fields is simple enough - an elysian Greek facade, so typical of the architecture of the eighteenth century. It is the other side of the building, the side that looks out over the woods, which is the real eye-opener, however. It is in fact, a fake Roman ruin, being essentially dominated by three arches of crumbling sandstone, which are so cleverly executed that they look as if they are about to fall on you! "Unstable", "precarious", this "ruin" nevertheless has stood quite happily since the eighteenth century! It is so typical of its time. It was undoubtedly inspired by those once highly fashionable paintings of Roman ruins which, shrouded in dense vegetation, form romantic backdrops to pastoral scenes. A good example is the well known picture of the Caracalla Baths in Rome, of which Mowbray Point might almost be a miniature version. Perhaps it was inspired by Langley's series of engravings of sham Roman remains. Certainly the more overgrown the folly becomes the more "Romantick" it appears to be!

Entering the road, turn left then right onto a forest track (signed Swinton Estate). Follow the track until it turns right, at which point leave it and continue onwards, following a path alongside between the wall (left) and the plantation. On reaching the wall corner turn right then left through a waymarked wicket gate. Climb up the hill to a field gate, (top left). Beyond the gate pass through a stile in the hedge (on the left) and after a brief diversion to the triangulation pillar on Horsepasture Hill bear to the right of powerlines to a waymarked stile in the fence.

    Continue over the next field to another waymarked stile to the right of a powerline post (90° to the main line of posts) by a wall corner. Cross the next field diagonally to reach the road at the far corner. Turn left, and at the bottom of the hill continue to the next junction then uphill to Grewelthorpe, passing the Hackfall Inn en route. Proceed back through the village to the start of the walk.

    By the ancient earthworks on the summit of Horsepasture Hill, views stretch over the Vale of Mowbray to the Cleveland Hills. Below, the Ure Valley appears as impenetrable and inscrutable as before. I did not see the "Alumn Cascade", Kent's Seat, the "Rustic Temple" or any of those other attractions listed in the faded pages of nineteenth-century guides. I am sure they must be there somewhere (or at least what is left of them). As I trudged back to Grewelthorpe hot and tired I realised that my walk would be little more than an introduction to this fascinating place. Hackfall is a place you will have to visit again.

14: THE COOK MONUMENT AND ROSEBERRY TOPPING

An obelisk erected to the memory of Britain's most famous explorer, coastal views over Teeside, a folly in the guise of a shooting hut and the lofty cone of Roseberry Topping are all visited on this upland ramble on the northern fringe of the North Yorkshire Moors National Park.

Getting there:	From Thirsk follow the A19 northwards to its junction with the A172 near Ingleby Arncliffe. Follow the A172 to Stokesley then the A173 to Great Ayton. At Great Ayton turn right and follow the road through the village signed to the station. After crossing the railway continue onwards past the station along Dikes Lane. Beyond a crossroads the lane leads up to Gribdale Terrace and then winds steeply to the left before ascending to the cattle-grid at Gribdale Gate. Here there is ample parking and access to a number of well trodden footpaths.
Distance:	6 miles. Lots of ascent and descent!
Map ref:	NZ 593 110 Outdoor Leisure 26
Rating:	Walk *** General Interest ***

The Cook Monument is the northernmost of the follies visited in this book. Southwards are the Cleveland Hills, with the high scarp of Cringle End particularly in view. This is where upland North Yorkshire falls away to the flat, industrialised coastal plain of Teeside. The Cleveland Hills, (gradually giving way to the high level moorland plateau of the North Yorkshire Moors beyond Hasty Bank), form the main upland massif of this area, Roseberry Topping and its surrounding hills being mere outliers.

From the parking area by the cattle-grid at Gribdale Gate an obvious and wide track (signed Cleveland Way) leads up through a pine forest onto Easby Moor and proceeds without complication to the Cook Monument.

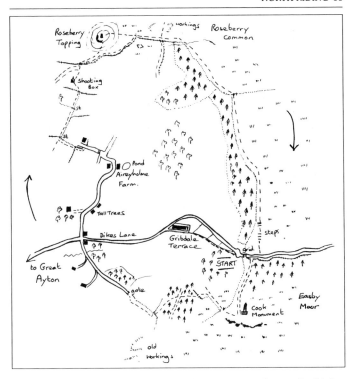

An iron fence surrounds the Cook Monument, beyond which a plaque bears the following information:

IN MEMORY OF
THE CELEBRATED CIRCUMNAVIGATOR
Capt. JAMES COOK F.R.S.
A MAN IN NAUTICAL KNOWLEDGE INFERIOR TO NONE
IN ZEAL,PRUDENCE AND ENERGY SUPERIOR TO MOST
REGARDLESS OF DANGER HE OPENED AN INTERCOURSE
WITH THE FRIENDLY ISLES AND OTHER PARTS
OF THE SOUTHERN HEMISPHERE.
HE WAS BORN AT MARTON OCT.27TH 1728
AND MASSACRED AT OWYHEE FEB 14th 1779
TO THE INEXPRESSIBLE GRIEF OF HIS COUNTRYMEN.

WHILE THE ART OF NAVIGATION SHALL BE CULTIVATED
AMONG MEN,WHILE THE SPIRIT OF ENTERPRISE,
COMMERCE AND PHILANTHROPY SHALL ANIMATE THE
SONS OF BRITAIN, WHILE IT SHALL BE DEEMED
THE HONOUR OF A CHRISTIAN NATION TO SPREAD
CIVILISATION AND THE BLESSINGS OF THE
CHRISTIAN FAITH AMONG PAGAN AND SAVAGE TRIBES,
SO LONG WILL THE NAME OF CAPTAIN COOK
STAND OUT AMONG THE MOST CELEBRATED
AND MOST ADMIRED BENEFACTORS OF THE HUMAN RACE.

As a token of respect for
and admiration of that great man
this monument was erected by
ROBERT CAMPION ESQUIRE OF WHITBY.
AD 1827.

By permission of the owner of the Easby Estate,
J.J. EMERSON ESQR. it was restored
in 1895, by the readers of the
NORTH EASTERN DAILY GAZETTE.

The story of James Cook is a stirring one. As the plaque tells us, he was born in Great Ayton and went to school there, working on his father's farm until the age of seventeen when he became apprenticed to a grocer in Staithes. Cook was not happy there and in July 1746, helped by his master, he was apprenticed to John and Henry Walker of Whitby...Shipowners. Cook never looked back. His first two years at sea were spent on the collier brig *Freelove* trading between Newcastle and London. Within a few years he had become mate of another Walker ship, the *Friendship*, and in 1755 he was offered command of this ship. Cook's response was to join the navy as an ordinary seaman! War was imminent and he felt that prospects for naval promotion looked good. He was right. He served on *HMS Eagle* and within a month had become Master's Mate and his career was under way .

Cook was involved in colonial wars against the French, and while in Canada charted the St Laurence and Newfoundland and earned a reputation as a gifted and meticulous cartographer and an able and zealous commander. In 1762 he married Elizabeth Batts at

*The Cook
Monument*

Barking. He was 34 and she 21. Now a warrant officer, he took up residence in London. While serving in Canada in 1766 Cook made a detailed report of a solar eclipse he had observed off Newfoundland. This was published by the Royal Society, and brought his name to the notice of men of science. By the tender age of forty Cook was poised on the threshold of his career. He never could have realised the sheer enormity of what he was about to achieve.

At this time there was a great interest in astronomy. It was known in scientific circles that Venus would pass between the Earth and the Sun on 3rd June 1769, a once a century event. In order to broaden astronomical (and consequently navigational) knowledge and to help with the calculation of the earth's distance from the sun, The Royal Society proposed an expedition be set up to observe this "transit". To make the necessary calculations the transit would have to be observed from three points: The North Cape at the Arctic tip of Scandinavia, Fort Churchill on Hudson's Bay, Canada, and an island in the South Pacific - an area then relatively unknown to navigators. Two competent observers were to be sent to each location. Recommended by his former commander, Hugh Palliser, Cook got command of the South Seas expedition and in March 1768 the navy bought and fitted out the barque *Countess of Pembroke*, a Whitby built ship. She was renamed the *Endeavour*. Cook's voyages of discovery had begun.

Cook made three voyages to the South Seas. His first voyage, in the *Endeavour*, lasted from 1768 to 1771. The *Endeavour* put to sea with a group of artists, botanists and astronomers on board, the first ever serious scientific expedition. The chief botanist on board was Joseph Banks, and he and Cook became firm friends.

On this voyage Cook visited Tahiti, mapped the coast of New Zealand (which was then believed to be a continent!) and explored the coast of New Holland (now New South Wales). Cook kept his crew in good health and free from scurvy by making them eat sauerkraut and onions. It worked. After sailing all over the Pacific in robust good health, many of the party were fated to die of malaria contracted in the Dutch East Indies on the way home...but nobody got scurvy. Cook and Banks returned to England to a heroes' welcome.

Cook's second voyage lasted from 1772 to 1775. This time, his task was to circumnavigate the high Antarctic latitudes in search of "The Great Southern Continent" which it was believed existed there. Two sturdy Whitby ships, the *Marquis of Granby* and the *Marquis of Rockingham* were appropriated by Cook for the task. These were to be renamed *Drake* and *Raleigh*, but in the end sailed as the *Resolution* and the *Adventure*.

Cook commanded the *Resolution* (*Adventure* being commanded by Captain Tobias Furneaux) and Banks was invited to lead the botanists, but success had gone to his head and he had lost all sense of proportion. He insisted on redesigning the *Resolution* to his own specification, which had the effect of rendering the vessel unseaworthy. (He had added an extra deck to the ship to accommodate his party - which made it top heavy!) In the end Banks was rebuffed by the Navy and Cook had the *Resolution* restored to its original dimensions. So great was Cook's reputation for keeping "a happy ship" that almost all of the seamen who had sailed on the first expedition wasted no time in signing up for the second.

The expedition sailed from Plymouth on 27th June 1772. Among the ship's midshipmen were George Vancouver (later to earn fame charting the western coasts of Canada) and Dr Charles Burney, brother of Fanny Burney, the famous actress. Cook sailed south to the Antarctic Circle and visited New Zealand, Tahiti, Tonga and Easter Island. The *Resolution* circumnavigated the globe in the high southern latitudes in a vain search for the elusive "Southern Continent". The only land Cook encountered was South Georgia, which led him to the conclusion that if there was any sort of southern continent then it must lie beneath the thick ice at the South Pole itself. On returning to New Zealand Cook discovered that the *Adventure* had sailed back to England after an incident which had resulted in some members of Furneaux's crew being killed and eaten by the Maoris. Cook followed in his wake. The *Resolution* dropped anchor at Spithead on 30th July 1775. The voyage had taken three years and 18 days, and in that time Cook had lost only four men, only one of whom had succumbed to sickness! The *Resolution* had also gained an extra crew member: Omai, Cook's Tahitian friend - who had decided that he would come and see England for himself. Needless to say, Omai was an instant celebrity, and he travelled everywhere, even visiting Great Ayton with Cook. How the bleak landscape of the North Yorkshire Moors must have appeared to this tall, bronzed Polynesian is not recorded.

Cook's third voyage was his last. Once again he sailed in the *Resolution*, laden with honours and good wishes, quite unaware of the fateful consequences which lay ahead for him. Omai returned to his native Tahiti with fabulous stories about life in Europe, and Cook continued on his explorations. But for some reason Cook had changed. He seemed to lack that steely determination with which he had sailed through the hardships of the icy southern latitudes in pursuit of a mere geographical speculation. On his third voyage he was inclined to dally, to succumb to the temptations of the South Sea Islands, where in the eyes of the natives he was almost a God. It was that deification which was to cost him his life. As with all living "deities" there is always somebody ready to disprove divinity by the expedient of assassination. Cook failed to appreciate the true nature of the local political upheaval his visits had precipitated. In short, during sudden difficulties in Hawaii, he was forced to beat a retreat, and, urging his men to the boats, made the fatal mistake of turning his back on the natives, who would never have dared to challenge this "god" face to face. Cook was struck from behind, and seeing him fall, the Hawaiians fell on him with their spears and cut him to pieces. Such was the tragic end of James Cook. Cook's sons, like their father, were also fated to die at sea, far way from home. Mrs Cook, however, outlived them all, and died at a ripe old age. Cook himself had passed on to immortality.

Today, Cook's memory is enshrined all over North Eastern Yorkshire. His statue stands above the Whitby Harbour he knew so well, and here, on Easby Moor, is his monument. It is not unique. On the contrary, it is said that more obelisks were built to honour Cook than for any other historical personage! They are numerous throughout the world - particularly in the Southern Hemisphere. In England, at Chalfont St Giles, a "Cook" column topped by a globe is sheltered by a castellated arch. This was built by Sir Hugh Palliser in memory of his friend. Great Ayton now builds its tourist industry on its association with Cook. The tiny pantiled cottage which was built by Cook's father, who had carved his initials and those of his wife over the door, suffered the dubious distinction of being taken down brick by brick and rebuilt in Australia in 1934. In its place Great Ayton got an obelisk, a replica of one sited on Point Hicks, the first bit of Australian Coast sighted by Cook. The obelisk is built of stone hewn from Point Hicks, but one cannot help but think that Great Ayton got the worst of the deal.

From the monument our walk is a steep descent through forest towards Dikes Lane. Bear right, descending slightly, to two stone gate stoops on the edge of the hill. Continue onwards until the wall bears 90° left down to the forest. Ignore a path continuing along the moor and descend diagonally left to enter a conifer plantation through the remains of a handgate. The path descends steeply through the plantation and crosses a broad track before leaving the forest through another gate.

Entering open pasture, follow the wall downhill for a few yards, then turn right, following a wall to where a stile gives access to a pleasant path between hedgerows, which passes a small wood on the right, becoming a metalled lane leading from Cherry Garth. The lane leads without complication to the junction of Dikes Lane and Aireyholme Lane.

Hereabouts there are remains of extensive mining and quarrying still to be seen. Mining has been carried out in these hills since the 1760s right through to the 1920s. Alum, jet, iron ore, roadstone and building stone have all been exploited at one time or another. Today the spoil heaps, adits and tramways stand derelict and overgrown.

Leaving the crossroads at Dikes Lane, continue onwards along Aireyholme Lane, winding up the hillside to Aireyholme Farm (where Cook lived for a few years) which appears on the left. Bear left through the farmyard, and at a junction of paths, ignore the track leading right towards Roseberry Topping, and instead continue onwards, following the track towards Aireyholme Cottage.

Join the footpath which passes to the left of Aireyholme Cottage, and just beyond a stile in the wall gives access to a path which leads down the edge of two fields beyond which bear left up a gorse covered bank to The Shooting Box.

Now Roseberry Topping looms large, but before ascending, let us stop awhile and examine this second folly on our walk, which stands on a grassy terrace, almost at the foot of the conical "Topping".

The Shooting Box is less like a shooting box than can be imagined. It looks more like a gazebo. A plaque attached to it explains both its origin and its function. "The building was commissioned by Commodore Wilson of Ayton Hall in the late eighteenth century as a shelter at lunchtimes and during inclement weather during shooting. It was restored in 1983 with assistance from the North Yorks Moors National Park Committee." Nowadays it shelters cold, wet hikers rather than grouse shooters.

So we come to Roseberry Topping. From the Shooting Box, follow the obvious (and eroded) path to the summit of Roseberry Topping. (If you wish to avoid the ascent, simply follow the path alongside the fence which runs around Roseberry's lower flanks.)

The ascent is steep, but the view from its rock crested summit is breathtaking. The full extent of industrial Teeside lies beneath our gaze, as is the sea, and our eyes can follow the shoreline up towards Hartlepool. To the west, the Pennine Dales are in view, beyond the Vale of Mowbray. Roseberry Topping's conical form is not entirely due to natural forces. Standing at 1057 feet above sea level, the hill has been extensively quarried for stone, which has contributed much towards its present shape.

From Roseberry Topping descend to rejoin the alternative path by the fence. Continue onwards into a dip to where a footpath crosses the path by a National Trust sign. Press onwards over Roseberry Common, passing the remains of old mine workings on the left. After ascending steeply, the path bears right to a handgate in a wall hard by a plantation (signed Cleveland Way), beyond which prehistoric tumuli come into view.

There are reputedly over 10,000 round barrows and ancient cairns up here amongst the dark heather, bracken and bents grass. There are prehistoric hut clusters, earthworks, standing stones and stone circles. The 10,000 square miles of the North Yorkshire Moors upland plateau must surely constitute the most unspoilt monument to the activities of prehistoric man in Northern England. The place name element "Howe" denotes the burial places of these ancient chieftains, and if you take a glance at any horizon to the south-east of Roseberry Topping you will see the tiny bumps on the skyline that betray their presence: "Loose Howe", "Flat Howe".... the landscape (and the map) is studded with them.

Now follow the obvious (and mercifully level) path which leads alongside a plantation (conifers on right, open moorland on left). After some distance the path forks. Take the right fork, descending steeply down to the road via a series of steps. Bear right to the cattle-grid and the start of the walk.

Roseberry Topping &
the 'Shooting Box'.

JFJ '89

15: THE WHITE HORSE

Forests, limestone crags, a brooding lake, gliders, and sweeping views over the Vale of York characterise this attractive, but rather over subscribed walk to one of Yorkshire's most famous landmarks, the White Horse of Kilburn. Also (independently of the walk) we visit the charming little village of Kilburn, famous for its master craftsman woodcarver, Robert Thompson - the "mouse man".

Getting there:	Follow the A61, A168 or A19 to Thirsk. Take A170 Helmsley/Scarborough Road. Beyond Sutton Under Whitestone Cliff the road ascends Sutton Bank. Park in a spacious car park at top of Sutton Bank by a cafe, toilets, information centre etc.
Distance:	2¹/₂ miles. Easy but busy!
Map ref:	SE 516 813 (Horse) SE 516 831 (Start) Outdoor Leisure 26
Rating:	Walk *** (if quiet!). Follies & General Interest **

First the walk! From the car park and information centre bear left and cross the main road at the top of Sutton Bank. Walk down to the telescope and viewfinder and follow the obvious path along the edge of the cliff with fine views over Lake Gormire and across the Vale of York. Ignore the Cleveland Way leading off to the left and the descending path to the right (you will return that way!) and continue onwards, passing the glider club on the left. Bearing left along the top of Roulston Scar the track soon arrives at the eye of the White Horse.

Beyond the horse, descend right, down steep steps to the car park and notice below. Bear right, and pass below the Horse to enter a wide track leading into the pine forest. From here an obvious (and well frequented) path runs back below Roulston Scar before ascending Thiefs Highway to rejoin the outward path on the cliff top. From here retrace your steps along the Cleveland Way to the Information Centre and Car Park.

The White Horse is not strictly a folly, but no-one would deny that it is a curiosity in the landscape, and as such merits a place in

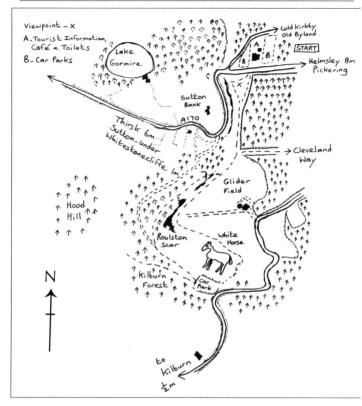

this book. Located in the Hambleton Hills, it is a landmark for miles around, being visible from as far afield as Rombalds Moor and Garrowby Hill. It can be seen from three other follies in this book: Harlow Hill, The Druid's Temple and Hackfall. The walk to it is easy, well developed and a must for all Yorkshiremen. The only problem is that if you want the place to yourself you would be well advised to visit it on a wet Monday in January, as the White Horse Walk in summer is a tourist attraction which tends to be as popular as Malham Cove or Blackpool's Golden Mile.

I found little scope for originality. The walk followed in this book is essentially a clone of the one you will find in the *White Horse Walk* information sheet, for the fact is there is no better route to the White Horse. If by some freak chance you are lucky enough to catch this route off peak, you will find a walk which is pleasant, scenic and rich in fascination. Perhaps, sitting alone above a high limestone crag, watching the ripples on a Lake Gormire the colour of the leaden sky, you will hear on the wind the whispers of ancient legend, and the romance which I sensed, but could not find amidst the clicking cameras.

The White Horse Walk starts at the top of Sutton Bank where there is a telescope and a view indicator. The view is phenomenal. From this escarpment edge 981 feet above sea level, you can, subject to weather, see the Pennine Dales, the Yorkshire Wolds and York Minster. Below, the Vale is a patchwork quilt of arable fields stretching as far as the eye can see. Near at hand, below on the immediate right, is the curious Lake Gormire, surrounded by trees, and faintly reminiscent of the Broomlee Lough which lies beneath Hotbank Crags on Hadrian's Wall. Gormire has neither inlet nor outflow and is, according to the geologists, a product of the last glaciation. The lake is aloof, mysterious, the sort of place you would expect Bedivere to throw Excalibur into. It seems a mystical place, the sort of place you would be not surprised to find legends attached to. You would be right.

According to one legend, the Lake is bottomless; and according to another it contains a sunken village with church and spire, whose muffled bells can sometimes be heard ringing beneath the dark waters. The most persistent legend however concerns a White Mare (which is not associated with the Kilburn Horse). On wild moonlit nights it is claimed that ghostly hooves can be heard thundering towards the scarp edge, followed by the chilling scream of a rider falling over the cliff. According to one popular account the falling rider is the ghost of a knight, Harry De Scriven, who, not content with his own famous black barbary stallion jealously coveted the white Arab mare of the Abbot of Rievaulx. One wild night he encountered the Abbot in a wayside inn, and thinking him drunk decided to take advantage of the situation. Inventing a tale about a dying farmer in need of help, Harry offered to lend the Abbot his black stallion, and having swapped horses the two men rode off into

The White Horse

the night. They had not gone very far however when poor Harry suddenly realised that the horse could not be controlled by him, and was bolting as if pursued by all the demons of hell. The terrified horse with its unwilling rider soon overtook the Abbot, and Harry suddenly saw to his horror that the horse was carrying him to the cliff edge. Hearing a mocking laugh behind him, Harry turned in the saddle, and just as the horse went over the edge he saw the Abbot, transfigured into none other than the Devil himself!

This is one version. Another account says that the White Mare was carrying a young girl; another says the Devil rode the horse over the cliff, Lake Gormire being formed by the crater he made when he hit the ground. The cliff behind is known as White Mare Crag and on the A170 is White Mare Corner. One theory suggests that "White Mare" is nothing more than a corruption of "White Mere" and simply refers to Gormire itself. I doubt this. The symbolism and imagery in the various legends point towards a pre Christian

Boynton Hall and its gazebo
The Carnaby Temple

Folly at Shaw Park, Holywell Green

origin. The Britons worshipped the horse and held it to be sacred (which is why the British still refuse to eat horse flesh), and the "White Mare" was associated with the Moon Goddess.

In Roman times the mare was identified as the Gaulish goddess Epona (who was also associated with geese, being the source of all the Mother Goose stories!). The legend of Lady Godiva, the nursery rhyme "ride a cock horse" and the word "pony" all have their origins in this ancient cult. The black stallion, the association with death and the devil also fit into the picture. The black horse symbolised the moon goddess in her dark phase the "night mare" or the dobby (again words that have passed into the common language, "dobby" becoming "dobbin"). The same religious ideas were endemic to all Indo-Aryan peoples (to which group the Celts belonged) so it should not be too surprising to find that ancient Britons had beliefs not unlike those of Hinduism (re-incarnation for example, which created a British contempt for death which was to cost the Romans dear). Our "night mare" equates with the Hindu Moon Goddess, who in her dark aspect is the loathsome Kali, the Hindu goddess of death. Celtic moon worship was matriarchal in nature, and no doubt it was left to later peoples to turn a black mare into a black stallion, a suitable mount for an Odin, or a Nikkr who in turn, with his satanic handsomeness, one eye and black cowl would become the prototype for "owd Nick" - the Divvle himself.

Many greater people than the Divvle have since toiled up the tortuous coils of the road which leads up Sutton Bank. (A mile long with four gradients of one in five.) John Wesley came this way, and recorded in his journal an account of the huge rock fall which broke away from the cliff with a thunderous rumble one day in 1775. The young William Wordsworth also came here with his sister Dorothy on the way to his wedding at Brompton, near Scarborough in July 1802. He must have liked the view, for he paused here again some months later on his way to Thirsk and took the trouble to write a rather flowery verse about it:

> I turn and view thy awful heights
> Stupendous HAMBLETON! thy dreadful wilds,
> Thy gilded cliffs and blue expanded sides
> at once infusing horror and delight!

The walk to the White Horse is a fine promenade along the scarp, with the added diversion of the glider field on the left, where we can watch intrepid flyers being towed up into the hazy blue yonder. Geologically the area has a character of its own. The crags hereabouts are of a yellowish corallian limestone, quite different from the white carboniferous limestone of the Pennine Dales. On our way towards Roulston Scar our path crosses a line of dikes, possibly once part of a line of Iron Age defences, although you will have to look hard to find any noticeable trace. Below, on the right, is the tree clothed bulwark of Hood Hill, where, legend informs us, the ubiquitous Robin Hood fought his last battle, and where in earlier times, druids carried out sacrifices in sacred groves. Here again, old beliefs raise their heads. "Hood" is a corruption of "Hod" which is but a variation of the more familiar Odin or Woden.

The top of Roulston Scar is not a place for the light headed. The dangers of this awesome precipice are appallingly obvious. At the base of the scar is a cave, appropriately known as the Devil's Parlour, which may be reached from the bottom path by those skilled in jungle warfare. A short stroll along the path, and suddenly we are standing behind the eye of the White Horse. Seen at close quarters, the White Horse is something of a disappointment. The eye is little more than a circle of grass surrounded by chalk chippings. Warning signs entreat the walker to keep off the horse, and a steep path descends down steps to a car park below, from where a more identifiable view of the figure may be obtained.

The White Horse was carved out of the hillside in 1857 by Thomas Taylor of Kilburn, who, inspired by the famous White Horse at Uffington, decided to finance the construction of his own White Horse. Taylor was associated with his brother in a London grocery business which specialised in Yorkshire hams and bacon. Thomas seems to have done the "travelling" for the business, and is reputed to have been at the festivities associated with the "scouring" of the Uffington Horse on 17th and 18th September of that same year. Taylor recruited thirty-three local men to carve out the figure, the whole project being completed by 4th November 1857. It must have been quite an affair. The village schoolmaster, Mr John Hodgson, declared a day's holiday, and both master and pupils assisted the workmen who were cutting out the horse.

Hodgson had apparently been given the task of drawing the outline of the horse, and appears to have been responsible for directing most of the operation.

A doggerel verse tells the story of the cutting:

> So he took his scale and compass saying "I'll do my best to try
> To make the horse quite big enough my friend to satisfy."
> And when the place was finished and everything complete
> He looked around the scholars sitting on the seat
> And called upon John Rowley, the biggest of the lot,
> Saying "Please do come and help to measure out the plot."
> They put in little stobbs and left them fair in sight
> To guide the men who cut the sods to do the work aright.
> Then thirty men of Kilburn, accustomed to the spade,
> All went to work so heartily that soon the plot was made.
> The school was closed upon that day and those who missed
>   their play
> Climbed up the hill to help the men to throw the sods away.
> November 1857 the White Horse first was seen,
> Dressed in a brand new coat of lime which made him white
>   and clean.
> A little girl when passing by in great amazement said,
> "O dad how will they stable him when he's to go to bed?"
> From Brafferton and Boroughbridge and far off Wetherby
> And right from York and Harrogate the White Horse you could
>   see.
> And scores of other places; and people in the train
> when passing to and fro can see him very plain.
> And stand upon his back on the hill so steep and high,
> And every year eight men do go
> To cut the weeds off as they grow
> For if he but neglected be
> There would not be a horse to see,
> And when the lime is washed away
> Instead of white it turns to grey
> So now and then there comes a time
> The White Horse needs a coat of lime.

The only hill figure of its kind in Northern England, the White Horse is in fact, as the poem indicates, an old roan! Most hill figures are formed by cutting out the surface turf to reveal the white chalk bedrock underneath. Unfortunately the underlying rock of the Hambletons is not a white chalk but a murky yellowish brown limestone so consequently the horse needs a continual supply of imported chalk chippings to keep it white. When the horse was first cut, more than six tons of lime was used to whiten it. Within a very short time downhill erosion and people walking on the horse had begun to distort the outline, and in 1896 it was almost obliterated in a rainstorm. As a result the horse has to be continually redefined and whitened. Initially the task was funded by Mr Taylor, but with his eventual emigration to Australia other sources of funding had to be found. No traditional celebrations accompanied the "grooming", but there is a story of the horse being whitewashed with "lime and beer". The process continues, for the horse constantly keeps losing its shape and colour, but mercifully there is now a registered charity set up to ensure that it is kept properly groomed, and this, combined with its present status as a major tourist attraction will ensure its survival well into the next century.

There are obviously no ancient legends relating to the Horse, but there is a modern mystery! How big is it? No-one seems to agree. Here are a few examples of the confusion:

No Through Road:	314ft long	by	228ft high
Rhea. North Yorks Moors:	315ft long	by	228ft high
Plenderleath:	40ft long	by	30ft high
Marples - White Horses:	304ft long	by	228ft high
Hartley & Ingleby:	180ft long	by	80ft high

Perhaps the real answer is that the dimensions alter minimally with each grooming (although that doesn't excuse Plenderleath). At the time of my visit large amounts of chalk chippings were being spread over the horse by a party of volunteers, and the horse was visibly bulging at the point where the chalk was being piled up prior to application. In the morning the horse was a dull grey. By mid afternoon he was brilliant white once more.

The walk now runs below the crags, a pleasant walk through woodlands eventually ascending back to the top of Sutton Bank by way of Thief's Highway. Kilburn Village lies a mile down the road.

If you are intrepid you will brave the tarmac down to the village and afterwards retrace your steps back to the horse. If not - well you can always drive down there in the car.

Kilburn is a lovely village. The first thing you will notice on arrival is the tiny little doll's house of a cottage which stands to the right of the lane. In some places you will see timber stacked for seasoning. This is hardly surprising, as Kilburn was the home of the famous woodcarver Robert Thompson, the "Mouse Man", who now slumbers in Kilburn Churchyard, but whose workshops still attract visitors from far and wide.

Robert Thompson was born at the Old Hall in Kilburn on 7th May 1876. His father (predictably enough) was a joiner and the local wheelwright. Thompson attended the village school and in his teens was apprenticed to an engineering firm in Cleckheaton (Thompson was to call it his "five years of penal servitude"). Travelling between Cleckheaton and Kilburn, Thompson would frequently stop to admire the magnificent oak choir stalls in Ripon Cathedral, which had been carved in the Middle Ages by a master carver named William Bromflett. Thomson was inspired by this work and dreamed of being able to re-create the artistry of that golden age of craftsmanship. At twenty he forsook engineering and returned to Kilburn to work in his father's shop. Here he made coffins and cartwheels and dreamed of the day when he might become a specialist woodcarver.

His first church commission came in 1919 when he made a pulpit for Yearsley Church and not long afterwards came his first big break, the chance to carve a large crucifix for the Roman Catholic cemetery at Ampleforth Abbey and College. The crucifix was to be carved in oak, and Thompson had no idea where he could get it. He roamed the countryside until he eventually found a gale uprooted oak on Brenk Hill Farm near Coxwold. Thompson bought the tree and cut it as it lay, the beams being carted off to his workshop. The Ampleforth order was a success and established his reputation and soon other commissions followed, it not being long before he was (quite literally) carving out a career for himself.

Thompson's trademark was his famous "mouse" which appears on all his church woodwork. By all accounts it originated in the 1920s whilst he and another carver named Charlie Barker were working on a huge cornice for a church screen. Charlie happened to make some remark about being poor as a church mouse and Thompson jokingly responded by carving a real church mouse on the cornice. The mouse stuck. Thompson realised it would make an endearing trademark, and used it as such thereafter. When quizzed by the vicar as to its meaning, Thompson replied that it symbolised "industry in a quiet place". "Nay man", the vicar replied, "it means destruction."

Robert Thompson carved wood into old age, and was still carving at the age of 79, dying on 11th December 1955. His work may be seen in 700 cathedrals and churches including Westminster Abbey and York Minster. His "mouse" may be found in schools, colleges, council chambers and even on furniture in country pubs! Thompson's business continues today, although one suspects that the old man, who once called back a collection of chairs because they weren't made from English oak, must be rather a hard act to follow.

Kilburn is a village of ancient lineage. Its name first appears in the following Domesday entry: "In Chileburne Archil had 6 carucates of land to be taxed. Land to 3 ploughs. Hugh, son of Baldric has now there 1 villane and two ploughs."

No doubt Archil also had a church there, but the present church of the Blessed Virgin Mary was not built until around 1120. Since then the church has been added to by successive incumbents. The North Aisle dates from 1170-80 and the tower from 1667. The whole church was "restored" in 1818. As one would expect, the church contains a substantial amount of Thompson woodcarving. Items of interest in the church include a "Breeches Bible" from 1601 (the text describes Adam covering his nakedness with breeches rather than the usual figleaf), and two fine thirteenth-century graveslabs, one of which depicts an Abbot of Byland or a Prior of Newburgh, and the other which shows the shield and fighting hammer of the said cleric's "Champion", who (priests not being allowed to fight) would settle disputes on his patron's behalf in the Norman Trial by Combat.

Kilburn is the home of a rural community, and has some unusual traditions. New Year's Day sees children touring the village in search of tips or tit-bits. This is known as lucky birding. Oak leaves are worn on Royal Oak Day (29th May), but Kilburn is best known for its Feast which is essentially a midsummer festival (St John the Baptist's Day), being governed by the first Sunday after 6th July. The Feast lasts four days (Saturday to Tuesday) and the festivities reach a climax on the Tuesday where a "Lord Mayor" accompanied by a heavily rouged transvestite "Lady Mayoress" tour the village in a decorated "coach" drawn by a "coachman". The "Mayor" inflicts small fines on householders and proclaims his authority for a year and a day while the "Mayoress" embraces and kisses any ladies he can get his hands on! Needless to say, everyone finishes up in the Forester's Arms, and the celebrations terminate with the singing of a strange song about "Old Grimy" which is (not surprisingly in view of what we have already mentioned about the area) a corruption of "Grim" - another name for Odin.

Retracing our steps to the Horse we rejoin the tourist trod and proceed up Thief's Highway back to the car park at Sutton Bank. If you have the time and the energy further well-defined trails lead off in the opposite direction towards Lake Gormire (full information and guided walks available at the Tourist Information Centre). All in all an attractive, scenic and interesting walk.

East Riding

16: THE CARNABY TEMPLE

Fine coastal views, two contrasting churches, an eighteenth-century temple, a Roman highway, a fine country house, a gazebo and a mysterious dry river bed are the attractions of this gentle Wolds walk to the valley of the Gypsey Race.

Getting there:	Carnaby stands just outside Bridlington on the busy A166. There are lots of narrow lanes in Carnaby, but no car park. You will have to use your imagination. Another option might be to come out by bus from nearby Bridlington, where there is ample parking (though free parking is virtually non-existent).
Distance:	3¹/₂ miles. Easy. Take the kids.
Map ref:	TA 148 655 Landranger 101
Rating:	Walk *** General Interest ***

Walk a few yards from the bustling artery of communication which slices mercilessly through the heart of Carnaby, and you will find a lazy, sleepy, gentle Wolds community. Although much of the area to the south of the village is now given over to industrial estates, on the periphery of the former Carnaby Airfield, built in 1944, the traditional nucleus of Carnaby still retains its rural charm.

Just 2¹/₂ miles from Bridlington, Carnaby is one of a string of villages which stand at the base of the Wolds, on the northern edge of the coastal lowlands of Holderness. Our route proceeds along Temple Lane, and within a very short distance we find ourselves climbing up onto the Wold with fine views of the Holderness coastline opening up behind us. Around Temple Farm, the soil is a rich arable brown, laden with fragments of chalk. Prior to the enclosures of the eighteenth century many of these vast arable

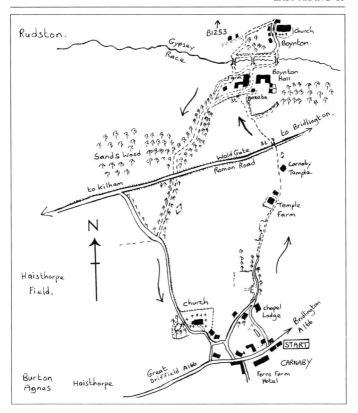

spaces were filled with the open field strips of the parish, while the low lying Holderness land to the south of the parish was largely moorland and scrub.

From the main road, proceed up Temple Lane to Temple Farm. Pass farm buildings on the left to reach the Carnaby Temple in the field ahead.

The Carnaby Temple is quite unmistakable. It crowns the summit of the wold, and from it there are extensive views. To the right, Flamborough Head with its lighthouse is just visible. This octagonal red brick tower, two storeys high and containing a basement, was built by our old friend John Carr for Sir George Strickland in the late eighteenth century. Probably built as a lookout tower, it was based on the Temple of the Four Winds in Athens. The four windows of the temple (now bricked up) faced the cardinal points of the compass. From the centre of the roof rises an octagonal brick cupola, crowned by a leaden ball finial. Inside, I am informed, there were once attractive frescoes dating from 1771. The chimney stack and extension were apparently added at a later date when the building was used by farm labourers. Eventually it became a storehouse, and then, after being used in the last war by the military for an undisclosed purpose, it eventually fell into dereliction.

The name Strickland is writ large hereabouts. As lords of the manor up to 1950, and owners of nearby Boynton Hall, they were to this part of the Wolds what the Sykes Family were to Sledmere, although on a rather less grand scale.

Beyond the Carnaby Temple we continue onwards across an arable field following a line of electricity poles to join tarmac at the Wold Gate, which marks the northern boundary of Carnaby Parish. This is a very ancient thoroughfare, being a part of the old Roman road system connecting York to Bridlington via Stamford Bridge. Looking at this backwater of a lane, descending the wold towards Bridlington in a long straight line with verges at either side, this is not hard to imagine. There were two Roman highways heading for Bridlington on either side of the Rudston Valley (which is the vale before us). The northern road was the High Street, which ran through Rudston, Swaythorpe and Sledmere. Our road (the southern branch) was known as The Low Street, and led westwards to Kilham and then onwards along Green Lane past Sir Tatton's Monument.

Very little is known of the Roman significance of Bridlington. Bridlington Bay is a natural haven and there would almost certainly have been some kind of landing place there. Roman pottery and coins have been found in Bridlington, some of them on the beach. Remains of a paved road discovered near Sewerby suggests that it might have led to a signal station on Flamborough Head. The original Roman harbour at Bridlington (if there was one) is almost certainly beneath the sea, having long ago succumbed to that gnawing erosion that ravages the Holderness coast. Very likely there was a fort or military base there also, although no Roman buildings have ever been traced. The mediaeval harbour which preceded Bridlington Quay was known as Castleburn. Perhaps this referred to our hypothetical Roman fort.

The Romans were not the first inhabitants of the area. Before (and during) their coming, this was the homeland of the Celtic Parisii (the same tribe that gave their name to modern Paris) and their burial sites and numerous defensive earthworks may be found all over the Wolds, particularly in the vicinity of these ancient thoroughfares. Around nearby Rudston prehistoric remains are numerous, and the mysterious Argam Dykes are second only to the even more ancient and mysterious Rudston Monolith, that enormous pagan phallic symbol which towers malevolently above nearby Rudston Church.

Cross Wold Gate to a stile opposite (signed) and proceed down another arable field to the boundary of Boynton Hall's parkland. Bear left, following the perimeter fence round to a stile. Descend pasture to the next stile (rear of Boynton Hall visible on right) beyond which a grassy track leads right, past a pig farm (on left) to the Boynton Hall Gazebo, beyond which lies the lovely mansion of Boynton Hall.

Unlike Sledmere, the whole area of Boynton seems much less 'private' and its charms may be enjoyed at a relatively close range. Turning the corner by the farm, the first thing to catch our attention is Boynton Hall's Gazebo. This castellated red brick structure was built in the sixteenth century, but around 1770 - at the same time as the construction of the Carnaby Temple - it was given a "facelift", acquiring its present Gothick features.

Boynton Hall itself has undergone similar facelifts. The original house was built in the late sixteenth century, probably by William Strickland (of whom more shortly), or his son Walter. It was from the outset a three storeyed building, being built of red brick and stone plundered from Bridlington Priory. In 1674 the house was described as having "23 hearths" (such records exist because at the time you had to pay a tax on each one). The exterior of the house was extensively altered during the 1730s by Sir William Strickland (d.1735), but much of the earlier work was left inside the new classical facade. The stone mullions of an earlier age disappeared during this alteration and were replaced by sash windows. Towards the end of the eighteenth century the house was altered for a third time, when John Carr was employed for the task. This time it was given a total facelift, which completely altered the original house, and added a range of outbuildings, giving it the appearance it retains to this day. This intensive work was carried out between 1765 and 1780. Today, Boynton Hall is occupied as flats, but its charm and grace remain.

Passing around the front of the hall we come to a series of ornamental bridges over the Gypsey Race. I am told the "G" in "Gypsey" is "hard", but I have never heard it pronounced so, even by people whom one would expect to know. The romantic sound of the name, along with the decisive blue line with which it is depicted on the maps, might suggest to the outsider that it is a sprightly babbling rill. If so you are in for a disappointment: the bed of the Gypsey Race is usually dry!

The Gypsey Race is one of the most curious watercourses in Britain, having a hydrology that is uniquely its own. To say that it is an elusive stream is putting it mildly. Once upon a time, long before the advent of the glaciers of the last Ice Age, the Gypsey Race was known as the River Ure. Flowing from Wensleydale, the Rudston Valley was its way out to the sea. Needless to say, things have changed a bit since then. The Gypsey Race rises between Wharram-Le-Street and Duggleby, flows northwards a short distance and then eastwards for 22 miles, passing through Rudston and Boynton to enter the sea at Bridlington Harbour. For some of its course it runs as a stream, but mostly it runs underground, leaving a dry riverbed on the surface.

The name "Gypsey Race" is believed to be derived from the Norse "gypa" meaning spring (the word "geyser" comes from the same source). Its curious character is due to the porous nature of the underlying chalk, which allows the formation of natural underground reservoirs. When the water table rises, water is siphoned up to the surface, and the normally dry riverbed becomes an angry torrent. Strangely enough, although not surprising considering the contrary nature of the Gypsey Race, this sudden eruption of water is more likely to take place after a dry season than a wet one!

Ignore the first bridge over the Gipsey Race (usually dry) and bear right (passing front of Boynton Hall) to a second bridge. Bear left down the road to entrance gates and Boynton Church.

When I was here, Boynton Church was beautifully decked out with flowers and fruit, ready for Hawker's Harvest Festival and the whole building was a rage of colour. The Church of St.Andrew stands to the south of the village, by the entrance gate to Boynton Hall. Of the original church, only the tower remains, the rest of the building having been rebuilt in brick sometime around 1768. The tower, dating from the fifteenth century has perpendicular windows and crocketed pinnacles. Little is known of the old church. In the late sixteenth century the chancel was reported to be "in wonderful great decay" and quite unusable in winter. No doubt it remained so until its rebuilding. The eighteenth-century church is a masterpiece. Where one expects a chancel arch there are instead two massive classical pillars, and the whole interior is painted a pastel green. A flight of steps leads from the nave at the west end of the church to a fine gallery. The east window contains stained glass of 1768 by William Peckitt of York. The whole atmosphere is one of eighteenth century charm, elegance and classical grandeur.

The church was again altered around 1910, the old box pews being replaced by modern style seating, facing east. An old sepia photograph on the wall depicts the condition of this church prior to the restoration.

The church is filled with monuments to the Stricklands. Boynton's most famous curiosity is the Turkey Lectern which depicts "a turkey in its pride proper". This turkey is the Strickland family crest, and must surely be the most unusual heraldic device in the land. The origin of the "Strickland Turkey" is even more fascinating. Sir William Strickland (who built the first house), had this crest and coat-of-arms granted to him in 1550 after having sailed from Bristol with the Cabots on an expedition to the Americas in pursuit of gold. Unfortunately all he managed to bring back was a number of turkeys, which nevertheless, having never been seen before, excited much interest.

Another monument commemorates a later (seventeenth century) William Strickland, who, although knighted by Charles I, took up the cause of Parliament in the Great Civil War. After landing at Bridlington, under fire, Charles's Queen, Henrietta Maria, sought sanctuary at Boynton on her way to York. She received a courteous but cold welcome.

From Boynton our route leads back uphill to the Wold Gate. Beyond the church turn left, following a track through houses (signed Public Bridleway). Bearing left, ignore a footpath leading off through houses and follow the main track. This leads back through trees to yet another bridge across the Gipsey Race (this time single arched with railings). Continue onwards, passing to the right of the same farm buildings encountered on the way in.

Beyond a small house the track leads up through plantations back to the Wold Gate. Cross the road and continue onwards, the bridleway becoming a long straight "tunnel" through overhanging trees. On reaching the tarmac road turn left and follow the lane which descends the hillside back to Carnaby, entering the village by the Church.

The Church of St John The Baptist, Carnaby, is a curious structure. It is like Boynton Church's "poor relation". Approaching the tower, there is a feeling of *déjà vu* until it suddenly occurs that this tower is a virtual clone of the church tower just seen over at Boynton. It seems likely in fact, that they were both designed by the same mediaeval architect.

Though less grandiose than its neighbour over the hill, I personally found Carnaby Church more intriguing. The first thing one notices on entering, is that there is in effect only "half a church". The mediaeval South Aisle remains but the whole north wall of the church consists entirely of eighteenth-century brickwork. In the sixteenth and seventeenth centuries Carnaby Church was reported to be in a ruinous condition, like its neighbour at Boynton, but being no doubt of secondary importance to the Stricklands, instead of rebuilding the church, they simply patched it up and this is the result! Restoration of the chancel began around 1680, and by 1719 it had been rebuilt in brick "in the coarsest style". In 1830 the original south porch was removed, the aisle was re-roofed and the brick clerestory added. New windows were inserted in the north wall. The latest restoration was in 1966 when the slate roof was replaced by tiles, and a new ceiling was put into the nave.

Underlying this mish mash of brickwork, tiles and timber is the original mediaeval church! The tower is fifteenth century, but its arch is of the thirteenth century, as is the south aisle, and the aisle arcade. By far the oldest artefact in the church is its ancient font. Norman fonts are fascinating; there always seems to be something distinctly pagan about them. The lozenge pattern on this one seems faintly reminiscent of the staring faces usually depicted on objects pulled out of prehistoric burial mounds on the Wolds (the tiny chalk "Folkton Drums" in the Hull Museum being a good example). Carved on the fabric of the church, both inside and out are other "odd" patterns, which seem to have an affinity with the lozenges on the font. We can only speculate as to their meaning and purpose, which could be anything from "witch marks" to games played by Victorian schoolchildren!.

Other carvings are less mysterious. An old coffin lid is built into the south wall, and there is a carved "mass dial" which was used before the advent of church clocks. But perhaps the most interesting inscription is carved on a pier in the south arcade:

HIC JACET / CORPVS W / ALTERI VPPI / BI HVMATUM
CUIUS ANIMAM ABSOLVAT DEUS

It does not take a great command of Latin to realise that the inscription marks the last resting place of Walter Uppiby, who was laid to rest here in the early fourteenth century. The name is an unusual one, but it is recorded that the Uppiby Family held land hereabouts around this time.

The earliest reference to Carnaby Church was sometime around 1148 when it was granted by Robert De Percy to the Prior of Bridlington. Carnaby's association with the powerful Percy Family made it a place of some importance in those distant times. On 3rd June 1299 another Robert De Percy obtained a grant to hold a weekly

143

market on Thursdays at his "Manor of Kernetteby". This right is perpetuated in the modern cross which stands at the bottom of School Hill. It is inscribed "Carnaby mediaeval market stone. Reconstructed 1968".

So, as we approach the bustling main road, we have reached the end of our journey. Only one monument remains to be discovered in Carnaby, but I must confess I did not see it. (Perhaps it is no more, because the source of my information dates from 1892.) In a garden somewhere in the village stands a small column which was erected by Mr H.Robinson Esq., in honour of Melbourne, a famous racehorse which was bred there in 1830. Find it if you can.

17: THE SLEDMERE FOLLIES

Two unique and fascinating war memorials, a stately home, an ancient trackway and a tastelessly ornate prospect tower are the high points of this tiring but interesting ramble on the rolling Yorkshire Wolds.

Getting there:	From York (ring road) follow A166 Bridlington Road via Stamford Bridge and Garrowby Hill to the village of Fridaythorpe. Turn off left and follow B1251 to Sledmere. Car park and picnic area are near the entrance to Sledmere House, by the junction with the B1253 Duggleby Road, opposite war memorial.
Distance:	8 miles. A long hard walk, much of it on tarmac. Not recommended for small children. (Note: As all the follies on this walk are by the roadside you could get round them by simply using the car. But you wouldn't do that - would you?)
Map ref:	SE 928 647 Landranger 101
Rating:	Walk * Follies ****

"To help to save the world fra wrong
To shield the weak and bind the strong."

Park at the car park near the Eleanor Cross by Sledmere House. Proceed along the main road (B1251), passing the Waggoners' Memorial on the left, and the entrance to Sledmere House on the right. Continue onwards, passing the Triton Inn and the Domed Canopy erected to the memory of Sir Christopher Sykes standing opposite the main gate to the estate. At the road junction ignore the B1253 leading off left to Bridlington and proceed along the B1252 (Driffield) passing estate housing and the Primitive Methodists' Chapel on the left. Just beyond houses a farm track leads off left. Follow this to the Castle Farm. At Castle Farm turn right, and follow the farm road to rejoin the B1252. From here a long weary trudge leads to the Tatton Sykes Monument on the summit of Garton Hill.

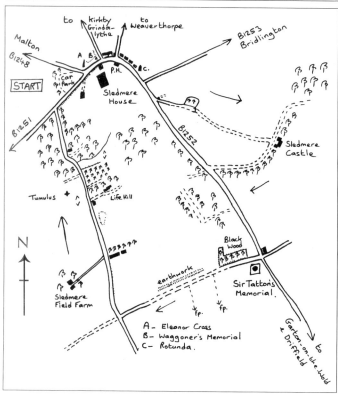

After examining the Monument turn right along a grassy track (signed Public Bridleway) running to the left of a stand of trees. Follow this long, pleasant promenade until encountering a metalled lane leading up towards two blocks of houses on the hilltop. Turn right up the lane back towards Sledmere, a long (and wearying!) tramp which passes Life Hill on the right to rejoin the B1251 leading into Sledmere. Turn right for Sledmere House and the start of the walk.

The story of Sledmere is the story of the Sykes Family, who turned a remote sheepwalk into some of the finest arable farmland in England and in so doing stamped their personalities irrevocably upon the local landscape. Our walk starts outside their house,

146

*The Waggoners'
Memorial*

which was first opened to the public in 1965, and which, despite the summer incursions of tourists still manages to remain a lived in family home.

Sledmere House, its black and gold gates guarded by Tritons, is the last of a line of houses. The first (Tudor) house was inherited by Richard Sykes in 1748. The Sykes family originated from Leeds and had made their fortunes from wool throughout the sixteenth and seventeenth centuries. Richard Sykes inherited Sledmere as a result of his father's marriage to Mary Kirkby, who was a descendent of the Kirkby family of Cottingham, and thus heiress to the Sledmere Estates. Richard Sykes soon made his mark. Demolishing the manor house he built himself a Queen Anne Mansion in brick.

This in turn passed to his brother Mark, who in 1733, as Vicar of Roos, was the only clergyman ever to be made a baronet. His son, Sir Christopher Sykes, really began Sledmere's "agrarian revolution" when he took over managing the estates in 1776, and after the death of his father in 1783 he turned his attentions to the house and park. Aided by the architect Wyatt, and the famous landscape gardener Capability Brown, he created a 2000 acre park which resulted in the uprooting of half of Sledmere village! Two wings were added to the house and the whole building faced with Nottinghamshire Stone, the existing structure being greatly modified. By 1787 the house was complete, and Joseph Rose, an associate of Robert Adam, was employed to decorate it. Much of Rose's work was lost in a terrible fire in 1911, but much was later re-created from original drawings by the architect W.H.Brierly. In the wake of the fire forty rooms were added (in brick) but these were demolished and cannibalised to build estate cottages after the Second World War.

Christopher Sykes had married Elizabeth Tatton, heiress to the Egerton Estates in Cheshire, and her huge wealth encouraged him to set out to "tame the Wolds". Enclosing the vast sheep walks, a treeless, hedgeless landscape since time immemorial, he put the land to the plough and made roads with large green verges to provide common grazing. He planted over 54,000 larch trees to act as wind breaks and built farms, stables and barns. By his death (in 1801) he had created over 34,000 acres of fine agricultural land.

His son, Sir Masterman Sykes (3rd baronet) established the Sledmere Stud in 1801, but it was his brother Sir Tatton (the 4th baronet) who really continued from where his father had left off. Inheriting the estates in 1823 Sir Tatton was to preside over Sledmere until his death at the age of 90. Sir Tatton was the perfect squire - the North's real life answer to Addison's Sir Roger De Coverley. He was possessed of an immense energy, and was a famous sportsman and racehorse owner. He increased the Sledmere Stud to over 300 head, and it is said that on one morning he rode over 63 miles from Sledmere to Pontefract for the afternoon's racing, overnighting in Doncaster and then pushing on to Lincoln the following day for yet more racing! On two other occasions he rode to Aberdeen for the Welter Stakes and then straight back to Doncaster to catch the St Leger!

One might be forgiven for thinking Sir Tatton a man of fashion and style, a fop, or a dandy - not so! He would work on his lands like a common farm labourer, with his coat off and his sleeves rolled up, hedging, ditching, breaking stone. No task was too menial for the energetic Sir Tatton. He noticed that the grass growth was more lush by the kennels where his hounds buried their bones. This led him to experiment with bone meal as a fertiliser, and to devise machinery for the purpose of bone crushing. He was man of many parts.

His son, the second Sir Tatton, inherited Sledmere in 1863. As a young man, his father had frequently sent him on long journeys abroad, basically to get him out of the way. His memories of his father therefore, were slightly less than fond. On inheriting the

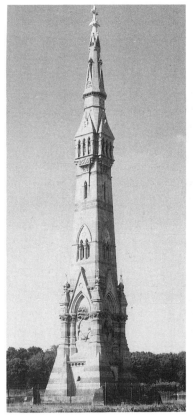

estates, young Sir Tatton wasted no time in instituting his own personal, somewhat autocratic regime. At Sledmere House he had the lawns and flowerbeds ploughed up and his villagers banned from growing the "nasty untidy things" around their cottages. For reasons best known to himself, he forbade his tenants to use their front doors, a bizarre and baffling measure! Young Sir Tatton however, did have his positive side. He was a social reformer, a builder of churches and a dedicated educationalist. He built five new schools, and, with the aid of the architect Temple Moore, rebuilt or restored upwards of twenty churches all over the East Riding, at a cost of over £2,000,000!

Sir Tatton's Memorial, Sledmere

The church at Sledmere is a classic example of his work. Only the lower part of the tower remains from the original mediaeval structure. It was rebuilt by Temple Moore in 1898. The interior is filled with fine woodwork, sculpture and stained glass.

Young Sir Tatton died in 1913 and was succeeded by Sir Mark Sykes, who was the last great builder at Sledmere. Young Sir Mark

Eleanor Cross,
Sledmere

was a famous traveller and diplomat, and had spent a lot of time in the Middle East. He had been involved in political negotiations in Arabia, Egypt and Syria, and had come up with the Sykes-Picot Agreement of 1916. A founder of the Arab Bureau, he was associated with Lawrence of Arabia, which alone was enough to give him a romantic air. He died (appropriately enough) while at the peace conference in Versailles. Above all, Sir Mark was a soldier, and it was as such, that he left his most lasting memorial on the landscape of Sledmere.

Having visited House and Church, we come to the main object of our visit - the follies. It might be argued that a war memorial is not a true folly, that the appellation might in fact, be construed as insulting when applied to a structure which commemorates the fallen of two world wars. But in the case of Sledmere's two war memorials, I feel we can make an exception. Without disrespect to their purpose their sheer uniqueness and eccentricity makes them worthy of inclusion in this book.

The main War Memorial in Sledmere takes the form of an Eleanor Cross. This is in fact a true folly, as it was not originally built as a war memorial, being converted to one in 1919. The original 'Eleanor Crosses' were of course built in the thirteenth century by Edward I. He was married to Eleanor of Castile, and when she died in Nottinghamshire in 1290, Edward in his grief vowed to build a cross to her memory at every place where her body rested on her way to burial at Westminster Abbey. Three "Eleanor Crosses" survive, and this Sledmere pastiche is based on the one at Northampton. It was erected in 1895-1900 by "young" Sir Tatton Sykes, the architect (predictably enough) being Temple Moore. It is 60 feet high and rises with a sweeping gracefulness from an impressive base of steps. After the Great War it became a memorial to twenty-three local men who did not come back. Sir Mark Sykes' "conversion" of the cross was tasteful, imaginative and (in a romantic kind of way) bordering on the eccentric.

Basically all he did was to add a series of brass portraits of the fallen, but these portraits are executed in such a clever way that they blend in with the thirteenth-century style of the monument and imbue the drab khaki and puttees of 1914 with a chain mail and armour imagery evocative of Crécy and Agincourt. Raymond

151

Thompson has a chained figure of war at his feet, two Sledmere joiners have their tools engraved in brass, and, in an eastern setting, we see Sir Mark himself with his feet on a vanquished warrior. Major Brown has an eagle at his feet with a small figure of Joan of Arc at his head. Each figure depicted has its own unique fascination.

A short distance down the road is the Waggoners' Memorial. Here, frequently noticed by the passing motorist but seldom visited, is what must be the most eccentric and unusual war memorial in Britain. War Memorials tend to fall into three basic types - stone monoliths, statues and mausoleum-like structures which range from the parochially minute to the municipally gigantic. The Waggoners' Memorial conforms to none of these. Imagine Trajan's Column in Rome squashed into a fat squat cylinder and enclosed by a conical roof and restraining pillars and you will be getting somewhere near the mark.

The Waggoners' Memorial is delightful! This astonishingly eccentric sculpture was designed by Sir Mark Sykes, who raised a company of 1200 local men to fight in the Great War. This memorial tells, in a manner worthy of Marvel Comics, their true story. We are introduced to the Waggoners with a series of verses, which are carved on mosaic tablets in a strange, sinuously fanciful script. As if to bind the spell, the verses are in dialect:-

> I. These steans a noble tale do tell,
>   of what men did when war befell,
>   and in that 'fourteen harvest tide
>   the call for lads went far and wide
>   to help to save the world from wrong,
>   to shield the weak and bind the strong.
>
> II. When from these Wolds XII hundred men
>   came forth from field and fold and pen
>   to stand against the law of might
>   to labour and to dee for right,
>   and for to save the world from wrong,
>   to shield the weak and bind the strong.
>
> III. These simple lads knew nowt of war,
>   they only knew that God's own Law
>   which Satan's will controls must fall,
>   unless men then did heed that call

IV.

to gan to save the world from wrong
to shield the weak and bind the strong.

Ere Britain's hosts were raised or planned
the lads whae joined this homely band
to Normandy had passed o'er sea,
where some were maimed and some did dee,
and all to save the world from wrong,
to shield the weak and bind the strong.

V.

Good lads and game, our Riding's Pride,
these steans are set by this roadside,
this tale your children's bairns to tell
of what ye did when war befell,
to help to save the world from wrong
to shield the weak and bind the strong.....

LT COL SIR MARK SYKES BART.MP. DESIGNED THIS MONUMENT
AND SET IT UP AS A REMEMBRANCE OF THE GALLANT SERVICES
RENDERED IN THE GREAT WAR 1914-18 BY THE WAGGONERS
RESERVE A CORPS OF 1000 DRIVERS RAISED BY HIM ON THE
YORKSHIRE WOLD FARMS IN THE YEAR 1912. THOMAS SCOTT
FOREMAN - CARLO MAGNANI SCULPTOR - ALFRED BARR MASON.

But the greater part of the story is told in pictures, for the whole
monument is a delightful tableau of larger than life comic strip
caricature. We see the labourers in the fields at harvest time, we see
them joining up, we see the soldier saying goodbye to his family, his
little dog jumping at his heels. We see the crossing to France, even
the mines and fish in the channel. Snarling spike helmeted Germans
burn a church and drag a screaming woman by the hair, as our
"good lads and game" arrive to "save the world from wrong". The
retreat from Mons is depicted, as shells fly through no mans land,
and grimacing huns fix bayonets with bared wolf-like teeth, before
being beaten and chased across a bridge over the Marne. Today the
"steans" still "tell of what men did", and one cannot help but think
that Agincourt and Shakespeare's Henry V must have been
uppermost in Sir Mark's mind when he planned both monuments.
Sadly, he died prematurely at the age of 39, and never lived to see
the completion of his monuments.

Sledmere's third folly is some distance down the road, beyond the village hostelry, the Triton Inn. Standing opposite Sledmere's entrance gates it is essentially a classical Rotunda (similar to that at Wentworth Woodhouse) which was erected over the village well in 1840 by Sir Tatton Sykes (the first), as a memorial to his father. The inscription tells all:

> This edifice was erected by Sir Tatton Sykes, baronet, to the memory of his father, Sir Christopher Sykes, baronet, who, by assiduity and perseverance in building and planting and inclosing on the Yorkshire Wolds in the short space of 30 years set such an example to other owners of land as he has caused what was once a blank and barren tract of country to become now one of the most productive and best cultivated districts in the County of York.
>
> AD 1840.

Leaving Sledmere our route follows the farm track out to Sledmere Castle Farm, which was built as an eyecatcher for Capability Brown's landscaped park. This is the oldest folly in the Sledmere group, being built by Sir Christopher Sykes around 1776. It was apparently intended as a dower house, but was never used as such. Informed opinion tells us that the house was almost certainly designed by John Carr. However, other likely candidates include Joseph Rose, Capability Brown and even Sir Christopher himself. Basically its façade is that of a castellated gatehouse with twin towers. It was first used as a farm around 1895.

The final folly in the Sledmere Group, Sir Tatton's Monument, is reached by a long slog (about three miles) along the B1252. Standing on Garton Hill overlooking Garton-on-the-Wold, this is without a doubt the finest prospect tower in East Yorkshire and one of the best follies in Britain. This lavish monument was designed by J. Gibbs of Oxford, in grey and brown stone. It stands around 120 feet high and was erected in 1865 by the tenantry in memory of Sir Tatton (the first) who had died two years previously. At the base of this grossly Gothic structure is a door, above which sits a bas relief of Sir Tatton on horseback, surveying his estates. An internal stairway leads to an observation room with oriel windows (the tower is not open to the public). An inscription, which runs as a frieze around the tower informs us that "THE MEMORY OF THE JUST IS BLESSED". The whole thing is crowned by an ornate cross on a pinnacle. Standing in such an exposed position as this, it is amazing that this delightfully ugly creation has remained in such pristine condition for 125 years. Across the road a stylistically similar house plays sentinel. Perhaps this is one of the reasons.

The rest of our walk is relatively unspectacular. The track which leads from the monument along the hillside (Green Lane) gives us a fine and undisturbed view of the magnificent Wolds landscape. Ancient history is writ large hereabouts. On these hills once lived the Celtic Parisii, and their burial mounds and earthworks lie all around, Green Lane running along the line of their defensive dykes. In their wake came the Roman Legions, who constructed two major roads (High Street and Low Street) across the Wolds, both of which passed close to Sledmere. Here, on Green Lane, we are actually walking along the line of the Roman "Low Street" which led from York to Bridlington. Beyond the Sykes Monument it led on to Kilham, and from there (as the Wold Gate) it led past Boynton to the coast.

Beyond Green Lane the rest of the walk is a weary trudge on tarmac back to Sledmere. In effect we are walking around the perimeter of the park. Tantalising tracks lead off into the Sykes domains, but all is private, and there is no scope for the rambler. In this respect the walk is a disappointment, and many people I am sure will be tempted to explore the whole thing by car and move on to more accessible countryside elsewhere (Carnaby being the most obvious choice). Only on ancient Green Lane do we get a taste of the emptiness of the rolling Wolds, along with a vision of days gone by as we plod along a seemingly endless ribbon of velvet turf. Perhaps this alone makes the BMW dodging worthwhile, but then again, if you parked up at the Sykes Monument you could walk Green Lane in both directions and get the best of all possible worlds. Folly tour and stroll? or long march? In the end the choice must be yours!

APPENDIX

Other Yorkshire Follies and Curiosities.

Allerton Mauleverer
By the A1 junction with the A 59 east of Knarsborough. Allerton Park domed garden temple.

Allerton Park
Domed Temple

Aske Hall - Near Richmond. Map ref: NZ 175 036 Landranger 92. There is a fine Gothick Temple, reputedly the work of Capability Brown, who is known to have worked at Aske Hall. Aske's greatest folly however is Oliver Duckett a "folly fortress" which was built as an eyecatcher for the house. Oliver Duckett is, essentially, a chunk of Richmond Castle which has been taken down stone by stone and re-erected here as part of a folly. It is basically a round bastion tower with gunports.

Azerley - Map ref: SE 266 742 Landranger 99.
A small castellated tower rising from a derelict Victorian House surrounded by decaying farming paraphernalia.

Barnsley - Map ref: SE 343 052 Landranger 111.
Locke Park Tower 1877. 70 foot high belvedere tower, erected to the memory of Phoebe Locke by her sister, Miss McCreary. Phoebe was the wife of a local worthy who first donated the park to the people of Barnsley. The initials S.M.C. may be made out on the weather vane.

Bradfield Dale - Map ref: SK 231 899 Landranger SHEET 110.
Boot's Folly, near the Strines Inn, SW of Langsett Map ref: SK 221 909. Situated in the northeastern corner of the Peak district National Park, Boot's Folly is a turreted sham "pele tower" with a flagpole which stands on the hillside above scenic Dale Dike Reservoir. Little is known about it. It was constructed using seventeenth-century mullions and masonry robbed from an old farm, Nether Holes, which stood further down the dale. Lying nearby in the heather are ornately carved neoclassical columns and dressed stones - possibly the building blocks for another, never constructed folly. According to legend the tower was built by a grieving widower so he could gaze across Bradfield Dale to the last resting place of his dear wife! In fact it was built by Charles Boot, the owner of nearby Sugworth Hall to entertain his friends! Boot was the son of the founder of Henry Boot Construction. The lower part of the staircase was apparently removed after being ascended by a curious cow which got stuck at the top and had to be lowered down on ropes!

Bradford - Bierley Hall Grotto. Map ref: SE 175 295 Landranger 104. The grotto is located at the head of a series of small fishponds in the little wooded valley between Bierley Hospital and the Euroway Industrial Estate (off the M606). I did not find the remains of the reported fake stone circle, but I did locate the dark and spidery grotto, its entrance cunningly hidden amid a contrived jumble of black boulders piled one on top of the other. These stones were brought here from the extremities of Wibsey Slack. Also of interest is an adjacent dam of "Druidic" looking boulders, from which a stream empties into the lake. The follies were built sometime in the eighteenth century by Dr Richard Richardson of Bierley Hall, whose father, Dr Richard Richardson FRS, planted the woods and built at Bierley the second hothouse to appear in England. (The first British hothouse was built at Orford near Warrington, and Richardson employed the same workers at Bierley.) The first Dr Richardson was a famous botanist and his gardens at Bierley boasted a collection of plants which was possibly the finest in the North of England. The now demolished Bierley Hall was famed for its cedar of Lebanon which was sent to Dr Richardson around 1705 by his friend Sir Hans Sloane, President of the Royal Society. Dr Richardson, the father, died in 1741, Dr Richardson the son, in 1781.

The grotto, though dilapidated, is well worth a visit.

Bradford - Undercliffe Cemetery. Map ref: SE 174 343 Landranger 104.

Contains a number of interesting monuments, the best known being an "Egyptian" mausoleum.

Brighouse - Robin Hood's Grave, Kirklees Park. Map ref: SE 174 215 Landranger 104.
Surrounded by railings, a stone carries a fanciful epitaph to the fabled hero of Sherwood Forest:

> Hear Underneath this laitl stean
> Laz robert earl of Huntingtun
> Ne'er arcir ver az hie sa geud
> An pipl Kauld im robin heud
> Sick utlawz az hi an iz men
> Vil england nivr si agen
> Obiit 24 Kal Dekembris 1247

Skelbrooke - Map ref: SE 519 118 Landranger 111.
Robin Hood's Well. This small, square building with rusticated arches stands beside the A1 at the end of a lay-by. It was commissioned by the Earl of Carlisle (of Castle Howard) and

Robin Hood's
Well.

designed by Vanbrugh in 1711 to mark the spot where the Bishop of Hereford was supposedly forced to dance after having had his purse purloined by the famous outlaw. A Monk Bretton Priory charter of 1422 refers to the "stone of Robin Hood", and the Vanbrugh Folly was supposedly erected on the spot. However, when the A1 was widened some years ago, the folly was moved and rebuilt in its present location. Now ruinous and fenced off with "danger" signs.

Burton Park - (north of Leyburn). Map ref: SE 155 921 Landranger 99.
A grotto and a monument - mysterious!

Burghwallis - Map ref: SE 558 177 Landranger 111 exact location uncertain.
Sutton Moor Tower and obelisk. History and origin unknown.

Byland Abbey - Map ref: SE 549 789 Landranger 100.
Belvedere Tower built for John Wormald by J.Dodds. Topped with iron railings.

Clapham - Map ref: SD 749 699 Landranger 98.
Grotto in the grounds of Ingleborough Hall, by path to Trow Gill and Ingleborough. Probably built by the Farrer Family, of whom Reginald Farrer (1880-1920) was an internationally known botanist.

Cottingham - Map ref: TA 024 323 Landranger 107.
In the grounds of Castle Hill Hospital, a Gothic tower of whitewashed brick, a hexagonal structure, erected by the Thompson Family as an eyecatcher for their now demolished Cottingham Castle. The house was built in 1815 by Mr Thomas Thompson MP, whose son, General Thomas Perrouet Thompson, was the creator of the enharmonic guitar.

Dallowgill - near Pateley Bridge. Map ref: SE 186 724 Landranger 99.
Greygarth Monument. A tiny roughstone tower, recently restored, it contains a new aluminium ladder. Its location is remote. The original (pointed) tower was erected by "ploughboys" to mark the spot where the last wolf in the area was killed. This was blown down around 1890. The present tower was built by subscription to celebrate Queen Victoria's Diamond Jubilee in 1897 and restored 1984 by the local parish council and Harrogate Borough Council.

East Witton - Map ref: SE 14 85 Landranger 99, location uncertain. "Slobbering Sal", also known as "Tilsey Folly", is basically a spring with a grotto-like entrance built by Marquess of Ailesbury in 1817. In woods on Witton Fell, difficult to locate.

Ebberston - near Pickering. Map ref: SE 892 833 Landranger 101. King Aelfrid's Cave and Sham Tumulus were erected as a memorial to Aelfrid in 1790. The Northumbrian King Aelfrid is reputed to have died of his wounds here.

Forcett Park - (north of Richmond). Map ref: NZ 173 124 Landranger 92. There is a fine Triumphal Arch lodge, tripartite with side entrances. It was reputedly constructed by James Paine who was responsible for a now lost temple in the grounds. A grotto and an ice house apparently still remain.

Garton-with-Grimston - near Withernsea. Map ref: TA 283 352 Landranger 107.
A mile to the east of this Holderness village is Grimston Garth, designed by John Carr around 1781. A Georgian Gothic creation, it was built for Thomas Grimston in the form of a castellated triangle with three round corner towers and a central hexagonal tower. The gatehouse to the estate was built by Thomas Earle of Hull in 1812 and is a massive structure, complete with turrets, battlements and portcullis!

Gilling West - Sedbury Park. Map ref: NZ 206 054 Landranger 92 and 93.
There is a fine Georgian Lodge on the nearby road, but the real "folly" interest is a rustic Tower by Foss c.1800. This stands on a rock outcrop about 20 feet high and is framed by trees. The lower storey is arcaded with Gothic arches and the upper room has pointed windows and a dome. A battlemented wall runs to each side of it. On a hillside above the Gilling-Barnard Castle road stand a group of castellated farm buildings built as an eyecatcher to the house. The buildings have been converted into a modern residence. With blank arches and arrow slits, this structure must have the most heavily fortified lounge in Britain!

Halifax - Castle Carr, Dean Head, Luddenden Dean. Map ref: SE 021 305 Landranger 104.
Ruins of a nineteenth-century manufacturer's country mansion,

Shaw Park, Holywell Green, Halifax

built in grand baronial style. Also two castellated lodge gates. Surrounded by moors. Castle ruins are on private land.

Halifax - Shaw Park, Stainland, Castle Follies. Map ref: SE 088 198 Landranger 110.

This public park was once the private grounds of Brooklands, which was the residence of millowner Mr Samuel Shaw (1819-1887), "a gentleman of benign influence", a prolific builder and a local benefactor. As well as teaching in Sunday Schools for over 21 years, he built the local congregational school, the church, parsonage and Mechanics Institute. Samuel was also a bird fancier, and the magnificent Castle Follies were originally constructed as aviaries. Samuel was the senior partner of John Shaw and Sons, whose woollen and worsted mills had been continually enlarged since 1782, by 1917 employing over 1000 hands and covering some seven acres. The mill complex, Brookroyd, has recently been demolished. The park (which also contains gardens, swings and an ornamental lake) was presented to the former Elland Urban District Council by Mr Raymond Shaw in 1955. To get to it follow the road from West Vale (see Wainhouse Tower) uphill towards Stainland. Turn left down the side of the Holywell Inn just before reaching Lodge Gates and Shaw Lane. Turn right to a car park, passing the Holy Well (improved 1843) on the left.

Halifax - Shelf. Map ref: SE 121 295 Landranger 104.
Lion Gate beyond the Windmill Inn, near Shelf Moor Road, a tall

Lion Gate
Shelf.

three-arched gateway leading nowhere, was once the entrance to a track leading to the hamlet of Upper Brackens. A story goes that a deal was made between two brothers to build this gateway, and another at the entrance to Upper Brackens itself. The first gate, complete with lion, and the second gate were built, but the brothers quarrelled before the lion for the second gate was carved. The second (bare) gate was demolished long ago, along with Upper Brackens, but the Lion Gate remains.

Halifax - Shibden Hall and Park. Map ref: SE 105 258 Landranger 104.

Behind the Hall (open to the public) paths lead to an artificial cascade and a curious grotto-like tunnel which leads beneath the adjacent road to a pond. A curious castellated tower on the hillside stands by the shaft of Shibden Hall's colliery. (Workings also lead out into the side of the nearby Godley Road Cutting carrying the main road to Halifax.)

Halifax - Withens Hotel, Cold Edge, near Mount Tabor. Map ref: SE 045 307 Landranger 104.

Gravestone with epitaph for two greyhounds Wallet and Dart (in field in front of the pub).

> Here lie the remains of Wallet and Dart
> Who in their last race made a capital start
> But their owners lamented, they never got through it
> For alas they were drowned in Thornton Conduit.

These dogs were drowned on 31st March 1891.

Harrogate - Harlow Hill, Prospect Tower. Map ref: SE 289 541 Landranger 104.

A "topographical observatory" built in 1829 by John Thompson Esquire. 90 feet high, in warm sandstone, it was equipped with telescopes, and was open to the public at 6d per head! In 1933 it was converted into a proper (astronomical) observatory, and was used as a lookout platform in the last war. Today it stands derelict and forlorn.

Hebden Bridge - Pecket Memorial. Map ref: SD 990 295 Landranger 103.

A small obelisk on the hillside overlooking Hardcastle Crags (NT), near Hebden Bridge, West Yorkshire. War memorial.

Harlow Hill Observatory, Harrogate

Helmsley - Map ref: NZ 605 829 Landranger 100.
At Duncombe Park is Duncombe Terrace, a drive with two temples: an Ionic Temple of 1730 attributed to Vanbrugh and a Tuscan Temple. As at Studley Royal, Duncombe Terrace uses an ancient abbey as an "eyecatcher" (in this case Rievaulx Abbey). Also Temple in The Woods and Nelson Arch. (National Trust, open to the public, admission fee.)

Hilston - Map ref: TA 286 338 Landranger 107.
Another small Holderness village, a few miles SE of Garton, is the home of Admiral Storr's Tower. This 50 foot high octagonal structure was built around 1750 by Mr Justice John Storr as a landmark for sailors! With a turret stair at the back, it was once used as a cottage. In 1976 it was reported as being a henhouse! Could be incorporated into a visit to Grimston Garth.

Hornsea - Map ref: TA 20 47 Landranger 107, location uncertain.
Bettisons Folly. A 50 foot high castellated round tower, reputedly built 1844 by a Mr Bettison, so that his servants could see him coming from a distance and have his dinner ready for him on the table!!

Howsham Wood - north of Stamford Bridge. Map ref: ??? Landranger 105 Location uncertain.
Octagonal Tower. Now greatly reduced in height.

Huddersfield - Lindley Clock Tower. Map ref: SE 119 181 Landranger 110.

Lindley Clock Tower

A tall square tower, with a copper octagonal pagoda-like roof. The tower was "erected by James Neild Sykes Esq. JP of Field Head, Lindley, for the benefit of his native village in 1902". It was designed by the famous Manchester Architect Edgar Wood. The sculptures adorning the tower are by T.Stirling Lee. There is a dungeons and dragons feel to the tower - like something out of a Germanic fairy tale. It stands not far distant from Nab End Tower (see walk 4).

Hunmanby - near Filey. Map ref: TA 095 775 Landranger 101.
"Hunmanby Gate" is an ivy-covered "sham ruin" with pointed windows.

Ilton - Map ref: SE 153 757 Landranger 99.
Arnagill Tower (not far from the Druid's Temple), dating from 1824 has three windows and a door. About ten feet from the ground the walls were roughly stopped to simulate a ruin.

Keighley - Map ref: SE 049 431 Landranger 104.
Steeton Tower. Victorian Mansion with 'baronial tower'

Kildwick - Map ref: SE 012 459 Landranger 104.
Churchyard, an organ-shaped monument, erected to the memory of John Laycock, organist.

Knaresborough - Map ref: SE 351 565 Landranger 104.
Fort Montague, a house carved out of the cliffs of the Nidd gorge, stands above The Chapel of Our Lady of the Crag, also hewn out of solid rock. Both are open to the public (admission fee).

Langsett - Hartcliff Tower. Map ref: SE 225 018 Landranger 110.
On private land in a field beside the back lane over to Penistone, by Hartcliff Lodge is a small

'Organ' Memorial, Kildwick

round, rough-stone tower. Designed by Mr Askham of Thurlstone it was apparently built in 1851 for Captain John Ramsden, a local man who had served in the East India Company. Unfortunately this man died in 1841! Here is a mystery.

Leeds - Apperley Bridge. Map ref: SE 196 383 Landranger 104.
Elam's Tower, Woodhouse Grove School Grounds, near Apperley Bridge, between Leeds and Bradford is vandalised.

Leeds - Cardigan Road. Map ref: SE 277 358 Landranger 104.
Bear Pit. Once part of Leeds Zoological and Botanical Gardens which was opened on 8th July 1840 by William Billington and Edward Davis. The original gardens were around 20 acres in extent with lodges, greenhouses, bridges, ponds and conservatories. The bears could be viewed from the top of the castellated twin towers or through the portcullis, beyond which they lived in a brick-lined pit

sunk into the hill. Once upon a time there were brass bands, recitals and firework displays. The success of the gardens however, was short lived, for by 1848 they had been sold off, being finally demolished in 1858. Today only the ruinous Bear Pit remains.

Leeds - Map ref: SE 335 385 Landranger 104.
Roundhay Park. Hermitage and Sham Castle.

Leeds - Weetwood Hall. Map ref: SE 271 381 Landranger 104.
Small grotto.

The Hermitage, Falling Foss, Littlebeck

Leyburn - Map ref: SE 111 908 Landranger 99.

A fine Sham Castle, but badly neglected, stands at the back of Thornborough Hall (now the rural district council offices). It consists of two squat round half-towers with a wall between. In the wall is a big blind arch, a pointed door and windows. A path goes to the grassy top, where one can sit on a seat by the pinnacle of the folly - a hexagonal tower made of small stones. Inside is a curious vaulted room. Thornborough Hall was built in 1863 by Joseph Hansom, inventor of the Hansom Cab. The folly appears to be older.

Littlebeck - The Hermitage, near Robin Hoods Bay. Map ref: NZ 885 039 Landranger 94.

Falling Foss is a fine wooded glen with a waterfall and nature trails. The Hermitage is carved out of a massive natural boulder, and contains a large chamber with a circular seat capable of holding twenty persons. Inside is an impressive reverberation. It was built by (or for) a village schoolmaster, George Chubb, of Littlebeck, around 1790. The date and Chubb's initials are carved above the pointed door. On top of the boulder are carved two stone chairs.

Marske - near Richmond. The Hutton Monument. Map ref: SE 099 998 Landranger 99.

A large obelisk in a lovely setting.

Malton - Castle Howard. Map ref: SE 720 700 Landranger 100.

TV's "Brideshead Revisited", this magnificent house built for Charles Howard, 3rd Earl of Carlisle by playwright Vanbrugh, has follies in its grounds. Notable examples are the Carrmire Gate (1725), Vanbrugh's "fortified walls", the Temple of the Four Winds, the Hawksmoor Pyramid and the gigantic circular Hawksmoor Mausoleum, the burial place of the 3rd Earl. Castle Howard is open to the public (admission charge).

Mirfield - Dumb Steeple. Map ref: SE 178 211 Landranger 104.

Between Huddersfield and Dewsbury near Mirfield, beside a busy roundabout at junction of A62 and A644 trunk roads not far from Colne Bridge. A square column with a stone ball on top, possibly a boundary marker for Kirklees Park. Luddites gathered there in 1812 before setting off to attack local mills.

Nether Silton - Map ref: SE 456 924 Landranger 100.

In the Hambleton Hills. In a field near the church a great monolith

Bramhope Memorial, Otley

bears a cryptic inscription of which only the first letters of the words
are provided. Three lines are believed to mean:

Here the grand old manor house stood,
The black beams were oak, the great walls were good,
The walls of the east wing are hidden here
As to the meaning of the rest - the puzzle remains! -
ATCLABWHEY
AD1765
AWPSAYAA

Oakworth Park - near Haworth. Map ref: SE 035 389 Landranger 104.

Ornamental gardens of now demolished mansion built by nineteenth-century industrialist Sir Isaac Holden (1807-97). The site which is now a public park, contains a series of excellent grottoes, a summerhouse and a sham fossil tree!

Otley Churchyard - Map ref: SE 202 454 Landranger 104.

Monument to Bramhope Tunnel Builders, shaped like a railway tunnel.

Pateley Bridge - Yorkes Folly. Map ref: SE 158 636 Landranger 99.

The walk along Guisecliff is one of the most popular walks in Yorkshire, but Yorke's Folly itself is disappointing, being little more than two stoops of ruined masonry. What was once a fine landmark was wrecked in a severe storm in November 1893, and has deteriorated ever since. It was built in 1740 by John Yorke of Bewerley Hall - a "Rhineland castle" to provide work for the unemployed! According to one local source John Yorke's wife was German and was quite homesick, and so the eyecatcher was built for her - to remind her of home.

Queensbury - near Bradford. Albert Fountain. Map ref: SE 103 303 Landranger 104 .

Standing at 1100 feet above sea level between Bradford and Halifax, Queensbury is one of the highest communities in Britain and the home of the famed Black Dyke Mills Band. At the crossroads with the Brighouse and Denholme Road by the entrance to John Foster's mill stands the Albert Fountain, which was built in the style of the thirteenth century by Foster's in memory of the Prince Consort. The fountain was opened on 26th May 1863, on the same day that the village changed its name to "Queensbury" from "Queenshead". It was an day of great celebration.

Rawdon - Cragg Woods, near Leeds. Map ref: SE 205 389 Landranger 104.

Domed Retreat. A summer house. Origin unknown.

Richmond - Map ref: NZ 167 007 Landranger 92.

Temple Lodge, a castellated mansion, built by John Yorke in 1769. Nearby stands the Culloden Tower, erected to commemorate the Jacobite defeat in 1746. It is a very early example of the Gothic style.

This magnificent building is now in the hands of the Landmark Trust.

Richmond - Map ref: NZ 169 065 Landranger 92, exact location uncertain.
Hartforth Hall, north of Richmond - a castellated farm and cottage.

Rievaulx Terrace - Map ref: SE 578 847 Landranger 100.
Part of Duncombe Park. Terrace and two temples.

Robin Hood's Bay - Map ref: NZ 944 028 Landranger 94.
Fyling Old Hall has a pigsty with a classical facade! It was constructed around 1883 by Squire Barry of Fyling Hall, a much travelled man who brought home exotic plants, who had a penchant for equally exotic architecture. The pigsty has pillars, an ornate portico, a fluted frieze and an acanthus leaf drainpipe. The windows are Egyptian in style!

Rotherham - Map ref: SK 438 895? Landranger 111, location uncertain.
Boston Castle. A square, crenellated shooting box standing in the Rother Valley, 1 mile south of Rotherham. Erected by the 3rd Earl of Effingham to commemorate the Boston Tea Party. (Effingham was a whig, and sympathetic to the grievances of the American colonists.)

Scampston Hall - near Malton. Map ref: SE 865 755 Landranger 101.
Classical bridge, pavilion and castellated deer house. Created for Sir William St Quentin around 1772 by Capability Brown.

Scarborough - Map ref: TA 04 86 Landranger 101 exact location uncertain.
Baron Albert's Tower stands to south of town. Ruinous, it was built by Albert Denison, 1st Baron Londesborough, President of British Archaeological Association. In Peaseholme Park is a Japanese Pagoda designed by George W. Alderson in 1929.

Scarborough - Map ref: TA 048 895 Landranger 101.
Marine Drive: "Hairy Bob's Cave". Not a hermitage, but a rock shelter carved out by navvies during the construction of the Marine Drive in the late nineteenth century.

Sharrow - near Ripon. Map ref: SE 328 722 Landranger 99.
Graveyard contains a pyramid which marks the grave of Charles

Piazzi Smyth, one time Astronomer Royal of Scotland.

Silsden - Cringles Prospect Tower. Map ref: SE 049 487 Landranger 104.

On Rombalds Moor in a field beside A6034 Silsden to Addingham Road. A tall thin tower, a bit like a leadmine chimney. Entrance bricked up.

Studley Royal - Map ref: SE 281 687 Landranger 99. Near Fountains Abbey, Ripon.

Gardens and terraces laid out in the valley of the River Skell by John Aislabie, his son William and their gardener William Fisher, for a house now demolished. Numerous follies - Campbell's Banqueting House (1729), Octagon Tower, Temple of Piety, Temple of Fame and the Roman Pill Box. Studley Royal now belongs to the National Trust.

Tadcaster - Grimston Park Tower. Map ref: SE 493 408 Landranger 105.

Grimston Park was built in 1839 by Sir John Hobart Caradoc, 2nd Baron Howden. It later became the residence of John Fielden JP of Todmorden, (see *The Fielden Trail*). A tapering Italianate tower stands near the house with a dome and flagpole.

Hazlewood Castle, a mile distant, is a small octagonal tower built in the 1760s.

Wentworth Castle - Stainborough Castle. Map ref: SE 319 034 Landranger 110.

On a hill west of the house. Sham Castle built by the 1st Earl of Strafford (of the second creation) who died in 1739. Was a circular enclosure with four square towers, and big castellated gatehouse with four round towers. In the central enclosure was erected a statue of the Earl by Rysbrack (1730). Only the SE tower still stands, others having collapsed in 1962. An obelisk, erected in 1734 to Queen Anne, stands west of South Terrace. A rotunda (1739) has 12 Ionic columns and was last reported as being in ruins. Another obelisk is to Lady Mary Wortley Montagu, a neighbour, who was responsible for the introduction of the smallpox vaccine into England in 1720. Umbrello - an imitation of the Chichester Market Cross erected in Menagerie Wood in 1759 - was designed by the "Strawberry Hill Committee of Taste", Horace Walpole and his friend Richard Bentley. Steeple Lodge, a fake church with a Gothic tower, stands near the entrance to the house. There were other follies, but most have been lost. An area worthy of detailed investigation.

West Witton - Wensleydale. Map ref: SE 085 882 Landranger 99.

High on the hillside by Mount Park stands Polly Peacham's Tower. This eighteenth-century structure was built by the third Duke of Bolton for the actress Lavinia Fenton, his mistress, whom he later married. (Polly Peacham is a character from Gay's *Beggar's Opera*). It was apparently built as a place where she could practise her singing. The tower is miles from anywhere - she must have had a lousy voice!

Wold Newton - Map ref: TA 038 721 Landranger 101.

Between two trees in a field ³/₄ mile to the SW of the village a brick obelisk bears the following (now almost illegible) inscription:

Here
On this spot, December 13, 1795
Fell from the atmosphere
An extraordinary stone,
In breadth twenty-eight inches
In length thirty-six inches
And
Whose weight was fifty-six pounds.
This column
In memory of it
Was erected by
Edward Topham
1799

Wragby - Nostell Priory (NT). Map ref: SE 404 175 Landranger 111.
Built by the James Paine and Robert Adam for the Winn Family. A pyramid lodge "the Needle's Eye", and a polygonal keeper's lodge "The Menagerie" with crenellations. Open to public at selected times. Admission charge.

BIBLIOGRAPHY

Adkinson, Philip "Erringden Deer Leap", *Dalesman Magazine* November 1979

Allison, K.J. *History of the County of York East Riding* Vol II, 1974

Baigent, Leigh & Lincoln *The Holy Blood & The Holy Grail* Corgi 1982

Bulmer *Bulmer's History of East Yorkshire* 1892

[Calderdale] *A Remarkable Tower. Centenary edition* Calderdale MBC 1979

Carter, Robert A. *Yorkshire Churches* Yorkshire Arts Association 1976

Clark, Mary Kitson *A Gazetteer of Roman Remains in East Yorkshire* Yorkshire Antiquities Society 1935

Cudworth, William *Round About Bradford* Brear, Bradford 1876

Dodd, E.E. *Bingley. A Yorks Town Thro Nine Centuries* M.T.D. Rigg 1958

Dyson Taylor, M.A. *History of Huddersfield & District* Alfred Jubb 1951

East Riding Antiquarian Transactions 1899

Elliot, Brian *The Making of Barnsley* Wharncliffe Pub.

Gaunt, Arthur *It's Odd - It's Yorkshire* Frank Graham 1971

Halifax Antiquarian Society Papers 1909

Halifax Antiquarian Society Transactions 1918

Hannon, Paul *Walks in Nidderdale* Hillside Publications 1985

Hartley, M. & Ingleby, J. *Wonders of Yorkshire* Dent 1959

Hawkes, Jaquetta *Prehistoric & Roman Monuments in England & Wales* Sphere 1973

Headley, G. & Meulenkamp, W. *Follies - a National Trust Guide* Jonathan Cape 1985

[Hebden Bridge] *Hebden Bridge - the Pennine Centre* Hebden Bridge 1976

Hey, David *The Making of South Yorkshire* Moorland 1979

Holdsworth, Bruce M.A. *Coiner's Chronicle* Peacock Books 1984

James, John FSA *History & Topography of Bradford* Vol 2 Mountain Press 1967

Jarratt, Jim *The Fielden Trail* Smith Settle 1988

Jarratt, Jim *The Watersheds Walk* Smith Settle 1988

174

Johnson, Francis F. "Boynton Hall" *Royal Archaeological Institute Proceedings* Hull 1984

Kirklees Museums *Castle Hill, Mystery & Legend* Info Sheet 7

Marples, Maurice *White Horses & Other Hill Figures* Country Life, London 1949

Mee, Arthur *King's England. Yorkshire E. Riding* Hodder & Stoughton 1941

Minchinton, Walter *Industrial Archaeology Sites in Britain* Granada 1984

Peltor, L.R. Revd. *Kilburn Yorkshire* Kilburn Church 1964

Pevsner, Nikolaus *Buildings of England. Yorkshire West Riding* Penguin 1959

Pill, David *Yorkshire The West Riding* Batsford 1977

Porter, John *The Making of the Central Pennines* Moorland 1980

Ramm, Herman *The Parisii* Gerald Duckworth Ltd 1978

Rhea, Nicholas *Portrait of the North York Moors* Hale 1985

Richmond, I.A. *Huddersfield in Roman Times* Tolson Memorial Museum Publications Huddersfield 1925

Rienits, Rex & Thea *Voyages of Capt. Cook* Hamlyn 1968

Savage, E.M. *Stoodley Pike* Todmorden Antiquarian Society 1974

Senior Wayfarers *Countryside Walks around Bradford* Dalesman 1981

Thompson, Jas "Thompson The Mouse Man" *Dalesman Magazine* April 1976

Thorpe *Thorpe's Illustrated Guide to Harrogate 1886* Chantry Press 1986

Toynbee, Margaret *Charles I* International Profiles, Morgan-Grampian Books 1968

Villy, F *The Roman Remains from Slack* Bankfield Museum Notes No.10 Halifax 1911

Wainwright, A. *A Coast to Coast Walk* Westmorland Gazette 1972

Walks in Wensleydale Dalesman 1983

Wensleydale - A Tourist Guide with Map Dalesman 1981

White, Geoffrey *Walks in Wensleydale* Dalesman 1983

Woolrych, Austin *Battles of the English Civil War* Batsford 1961

Wright, Geoffrey, N. *Yorkshire The East Riding* Batsford 1976

Yorkshire Archaeological Journal Vol XXI

Printed by CARNMOR PRINT & DESIGN
95-97 LONDON ROAD, PRESTON, LANCASHIRE, UK.